The Courageous Follower

The Courageous Follower

STANDING UP TO & FOR OUR LEADERS

IRA CHALEFF

THIRD EDITION

Berrett–Koehler Publishers, Inc.
San Francisco
a BK Business book

Berrett-Koehler Publishers, Inc.
235 Montgomery Street, Suite 650
San Francisco, CA 94104-2916
Tel: (415) 288-0260   Fax: (415) 362-2512   www.bkconnection.com

ORDERING INFORMATION

Quantity sales. Special discounts are available on quantity purchases by corporations, associations, and others. For details, contact the "Special Sales Department" at the Berrett-Koehler address above.

Individual sales. Berrett-Koehler publications are available through most bookstores. They can also be ordered directly from Berrett-Koehler: Tel: (800) 929-2929; Fax: (802) 864-7626; www.bkconnection.com

Orders for college textbook/course adoption use. Please contact Berrett-Koehler: Tel: (800) 929-2929; Fax: (802) 864-7626.

Orders by U.S. trade bookstores and wholesalers. Please contact Ingram Publisher Services, Tel: (800) 509-4887; Fax: (800) 838-1149; E-mail: customer.service@ingrampublisherservices.com; or visit www.ingrampublisherservices.com/Ordering for details about electronic ordering.

Berrett-Koehler and the BK logo are registered trademarks of Berrett-Koehler Publishers, Inc.

Printed in the United States of America

Berrett-Koehler books are printed on long-lasting acid-free paper. When it is available, we choose paper that has been manufactured by environmentally responsible processes. These may include using trees grown in sustainable forests, incorporating recycled paper, minimizing chlorine in bleaching, or recycling the energy produced at the paper mill.

Production Management: Michael Bass Associates

Library of Congress Cataloging-in-Publication Data

Chaleff, Ira.
    The courageous follower : standing up to & for our leaders / Ira Chaleff.
  — 3rd ed.
      p. cm.
    Includes bibliographical references and index.
    ISBN 978-1-60509-273-7 (paperback : alk. paper)
    1. Organizational sociology. 2. Organizational behavior. 3. Leadership. 4. Power (Social sciences)
  I. Title.
  HM786.C43 2009
  302.3'5—dc22   2009018738

Third Edition
14   10 9 8 7

DEDICATION

THIS BOOK IS DEDICATED to all those who have found themselves formally in the role of a follower and who acted on the courage of their convictions despite strong external pressure and cultural inhibitions against doing so. Most of these acts go unnoticed and unsung. An exception was a pair of courageous acts that occurred during a contemporary military engagement.

The first act was by a United States Army field commander who refused to follow his superior's repeated orders to fire because he believed the position was occupied by other elements of his own army. He was right, and by refusing to comply, he saved his fellow soldiers' lives from "friendly fire." The second act was by the army officers reviewing the incident. They recognized the commander's refusal to obey orders as an act of courage, not insubordination, and rewarded it with a medal.

CONTENTS

5. THE COURAGE TO PARTICIPATE IN TRANSFORMATION

6. THE COURAGE TO TAKE MORAL ACTION

I THINK THAT THE AIM OF THE PERFECT COURTIER is so to win for himself the favor and mind of the prince whom he serves that he may be able to tell him, and always will tell him, the truth about everything he needs to know, without fear or risk of displeasing him; and that when he sees the mind of his prince inclined to a wrong action, he may dare to oppose him and in a gentle manner avail himself of the favor acquired by his good accomplishments, so as to dissuade him of every evil intent and bring him to the path of virtue.

The Book of the Courtier, 1516
Baldesar Castiglione
Contemporary of Niccolò Machiavelli

PREFACE TO THIRD EDITION

WHEN THE CONCEPT OF COURAGEOUS followership began its journey fifteen years ago through the first edition of this book, the landscape across which it traveled was almost barren. Today, a growing body of scholarly research and practitioner experience exists on followership. No serious student of leadership can any longer ignore its essential counterpart.

Even more heartening is the application of courageous followership, and related models of exemplary followership, dynamic followership, or followership of conscience, in a wide range of disciplines. You will find these referenced and taught in fields ranging from education to law enforcement, in the private and public sectors, among clergy and military officers and many others. The twin competencies of comfort with speaking candidly to leaders and of leaders developing cultures that foster candor are increasingly recognized as desirable at all levels and critical at the most senior levels of organizations.

The need for a second edition of the book was driven at the time by a pair of developments. "The Courage to Leave," discussed in the first edition, was recognized as a subset of "The Courage to Take Moral Action."

I amended the model to reflect this and explored the range of available moral choices. The other significant amendment sprang from a spate of catastrophic organizational failures that materialized despite attempts by courageous followers to alert leaders to their likely occurrence. I added a new chapter, "The Courage to Listen to Followers," as a vital complement to courageous follower behaviors.

There are two major reasons for offering a third edition of this book. They may at first sound mutually exclusive but on examination are clearly not.

The first is the emerging power of electronically connected networks of people who form "communities of interest" to share information and organize for action. These are fundamentally changing the traditional power balance between formal leaders and informally organized followers. On the political stage we have seen mass movements electronically mobilize to sweep leaders in and out of office. In the social and economic sectors, followers have found the power to individually and collectively convey persuasive endorsements or register serious discontent about products, services, or organizations to large communities of like-minded people. Leaders can no longer ignore the efforts of internal or external stakeholders to draw their attention through established communication channels to issues they consider important. If leaders do ignore these attempts, they will find themselves dealing with issues in the much larger and unforgiving electronic public square.

At the same time that networks have become more powerful, the upper levels of hierarchies in large and global institutions are often more impermeable. Like their counterparts at all levels, senior leaders are struggling to stay on top of the punishing pace of change, the massive increases in electronic communication, and the continuous need for on-site and virtual meetings to coordinate complex systems in volatile conditions. The amount of information they can process and the number of issues they can address are limited. To manage the workload, many filters are placed between them and the hundreds or thousands of staff who share responsibility for the organization's mission. Technically, it is possible for anyone in the organization to reach senior leaders electronically, but doing so is often impractical, disapproved of, or ineffective. At times, it is also vital. How do we reconcile such competing needs?

To address these critical dimensions of contemporary follower-leader relations, I have added a new chapter in this edition: "The Courage to Speak to the Hierarchy." The observations and strategies you will find here reflect hundreds of hours of work with individuals at every level of mid-sized and large hierarchies. Without altering the original courageous follower model, which has now been the subject of several doctoral dissertations, this chapter adds a layer of perspective and strategy that supports the five core behaviors of courageous followership. It will help new generations find and navigate the boundaries between their informally networked power and the formal hierarchies they encounter.

This is the boundary at which the success or failure of leaders and organizations will often be determined. Courageous followers can contribute to the outcome, at times decisively.

Ira Chaleff
Washington, DC
May 2009

PREFACE

IF YOU SCROLL THROUGH THE SUBJECT CATALOG at the Library of Congress, you will find the category "leadership" and hundreds of books on the subject. You will not find a category "followership," and you will only find a handful of articles and books on the subject, tucked away under the leadership rubric. This is curious as there are many more followers in the world than leaders. Improving their performance would seem equally worthy of study as improving the performance of leaders.

I have been absorbed with the subject of followership most of my life, since becoming aware as a child of the systematic destruction of six million European Jews by the Nazis during World War II. In my heart, like so many others, I held the German people responsible, not just their leader Adolf Hitler. When I was seven or eight, I made up games in which I rescued as many people as I could from the Germans' death camps. It was never enough.

How could a whole country follow a vicious leader to the logical conclusions of his psychosis? This mass support for a psychotic leader may well have created the contemptuous association my generation has with the term *follower*.

Only later did I learn that one of the basic principles of Nazi ideology was the *Führerprinzip*—the leader principle—"One people, one Reich, one leader," which portrayed Hitler as the ultimate source of power and justice. In the *Führerstat*—the leader state—the *Führertreu*—those loyal to the leader under any circumstances—were the noblest of human beings. The leader was always right. Questioning the leader was raised to a crime of the highest order.

I also learned of the "White Rose," a painfully small group that tried arousing their fellow Germans against Nazi crimes. They quoted the philosopher Johann Gottlieb Fichte: "Thou shalt act as if on thee and thy deed depended the fate of all Germany and thou alone must answer for it." But this principle of accountable followership obviously failed horribly. It was not sufficiently woven into the fabric of the culture. How many other cultures would also fail if this trait were put to a severe test? How many are failing the test now?

In every age there are leaders and their followers who commit atrocities. At this writing, many people were mystified by the mass killings in Bosnia and by their feelings of helplessness to affect the situation. Why do we feel helpless to influence these events we decry? At least partially it is because the farther away we are from a situation in which power is being abused, the harder it is for us to influence it. Yet the closer we are to a situation in which power is being abused, the more we are at risk if we try to change it, and the abuser turns on us. Thus, the people nearest to the event often let it grow unchecked. And the people farther away wring their hands.

Proximity and courage are the critical variables in the prevention of the abuse of power. With these variables in mind, I have written this book for and about the followers who serve closely to a leader. While it might speak most dramatically to the inner circle of a highly placed leader, the principles apply to the close followers of a leader in any size or type of organization, and at any level of the organization. I focus on the courage required to take advantage of proximity, as only with courage can we act quickly and early to ensure that the leader's power will be used well.

If we practice being courageous in our mundane interactions with leaders, we will be prepared if one day we are called upon to display extraordinary courage in our relationship with a leader. By weaving the principle of accountable followership into our culture at every level, the fabric will become strong enough to resist the periodic attempts of individual leaders to emboss it with their own martial coat of arms.

But it is not just at the extremes of human activity that these principles apply. The fabric is formed and reinforced in every organized activity of society from the youth group to the workplace, from the church to the military, from the nonprofit to the corporation, from the local council to the national government.

As a teenager, I experienced the damage caused by the strong head of a youth organization who kept it alive through his dedication and energy, and simultaneously traumatized it through unchecked verbal and sexual abuse. In the socially idealistic sixties and human-potential movements of the seventies, I worked with groups dedicated to reforming the world and watched in dismay when their leadership's own use of power ceased to compare favorably to practices in the world they were seeking to change. As a management consultant to U.S. senators and representatives, I observe the difficulty many have in maintaining an atmosphere in which their staffs are willing to give them honest feedback about their leadership style. As a consultant to Fortune 500 companies and U.S. federal agencies, I see the inordinate weight given to a senior executive's slightest request, without regard to the effect it has on serving the customers who are supposed to drive the quality revolution.

The most capable followers in the world will fail if they gripe about their leaders but don't help them improve. As a follower, I am working to sustain the courage it requires to be honest in my relationships with leaders so I can tell them what they need to hear if they are to use their gifts effectively despite their inevitable human flaws. I now see that at those times when I have failed to provide a leader with needed perspective and balance, it was not for lack of perception but for lack of courage and skill. It was I who needed to change and grow as much as the leader. By not doing so I, along with the rest of the group, paid the price of dysfunctional leadership.

Like many followers, I am also a leader in my own right, and I am working to transform my own leadership attitudes that quash the creativity and participation of my staff. This doesn't come easy to me. Though I may wince, I find myself grateful when a courageous follower skillfully and tactfully confronts me and helps me visualize changes I might make to better serve the organization.

I first conceived the idea for this book while reading M. Scott Peck's *People of the Lie*. I am indebted to him for raising the issue of irresponsible followership in his graphic analysis of the shameful massacre and cover up at My Lai by American soldiers in Vietnam. It framed my long search for understanding of the subject. This book is the fruit of my informal but deeply concerned and protracted observations, reading, and reflection on the leader-follower relationship.

Though the approaches and techniques I describe in the book for changing our relationships with leaders are often simple, they are offered with the understanding that changing ourselves or others is rarely easy. I have tried to emphasize the need for compassion and mutual respect in our relationships as followers and leaders.

Please be a courageous reader. This book is designed as a guide and a resource; don't follow it in a rote manner. While I encourage you to read the introduction and first chapter to get oriented to the subject, not all the remaining parts will be equally relevant to your current situation. Use the subchapter headings to locate the parts that are important to you.

This work is based on my personal experiences with both men and women in the leader role and the follower role. In my treatment of any specific issue, if I was not able to keep it gender-neutral, I somewhat arbitrarily chose one gender for the leader role and one for the follower role and stuck to that combination for that chapter. I must acknowledge, however, that gender issues sometimes complicate the already sensitive dynamics in the leader-follower relationship, and I have not attempted to deal with them in this work.

I am also aware of the inherent cultural biases that may render the model I present less relevant outside a contemporary middle-class, North American environment. I hope that some of the principles I explore will transcend the limits of my specific culture and speak to the broader human condition we all share.

Ultimately, the work that must be done to create new standards of relationship between followers and leaders begins within you and the experiences of your life. I invite you to explore this subject in your life as I am exploring it in mine.

Ira Chaleff
Washington, DC

INTRODUCTION

IN MANY ORGANIZATIONS, there has been a movement away from the extremes of all-powerful leaders and powerless, submissive followers. We hear about "shared leadership," a helpful concept in softening the rigid demarcation lines often found between leaders and followers. But there is a limit to the usefulness of this concept. Despite the fact that many people experience visceral discomfort with the term *follower*, it is not realistic to erase all distinctions between the roles of leaders and followers.

Instead, we need a dynamic model of followership that balances and supports dynamic leadership. We need a model that helps us embrace rather than reject the identity of follower because the model speaks to our courage, power, integrity, responsibility, and sense of service. This book proposes a proactive view of the follower's role, which brings it into parity with the leader's role. Parity is approached when we recognize that leaders rarely use their power wisely or effectively over long periods unless they are supported by followers who have the stature to help them do so. Regrettably, recent history is strewn with examples that support this observation.

In many situations, no matter how much partnership or empowerment exists, the leader has ultimate authority and responsibility. The CEO of a business, the commander of a fleet, the head of a government agency, the director of a nonprofit organization, the bishop of a diocese, all have certain powers they retain for themselves and accountability that is not transferrable.

It is difficult to appreciate the external pressures on leaders until you have walked in their shoes, until you have had to make payroll, bring a squadron through safely, or respond to the outraged constituents who elected you. The internal pressures on leaders are often equally potent. "Ego strength," one of the qualities that propels an individual to leadership, is reinforced in ways that can deform it into "ego driven." If these pressures aren't managed well, with adroit help from followers, they can distort the leader's decision-making processes and interpersonal dynamics. Usually, the distortion will be in the direction of more authoritarian behavior and away from the partnering we desire.

How does a follower effectively support a leader and relieve these pressures? How does a follower become a "shaper" rather than simply an "implementer"? How does a follower contribute to leadership development rather than become a critic of leadership failings?

As in all human endeavor, many of us do some of these things quite naturally. But most of us can readily identify times we felt frustrated in our "second fiddle" situation as we watched our leaders make a mess of things, whether from the best of intentions or the worst. The increasingly egalitarian age we live in does not allow us to comfortably shirk responsibility and say, "Well, she's the boss!" We've grown beyond authoritarian models that strip followers of accountability. But we haven't necessarily grown fully comfortable with a new way of operating.

Most of us are leaders in some situations and followers in others. On one level we understand and fully accept this. You can't, by definition, have a world of only leaders! To think of leaders without followers is like thinking of teachers without students. Both are impossible. They are two sides of one process, two parts of a whole. Teachers and students form a learning circle around a body of knowledge or skills; leaders and followers form an action circle around a common purpose.

But on another level there seems to exist the deepest discomfort with the term *follower*. It conjures up images of docility, conformity, weakness, and failure to excel. Often, none of this is the least bit true. The sooner we move beyond these images and get comfortable with the idea of *powerful* followers supporting *powerful* leaders, the sooner we can fully develop and test models for dynamic, self-responsible, synergistic relationships in our organizations.

If we are to attain the empowerment we crave, we must accept responsibility for both our own roles and the roles of our leaders. Only by accepting this dual responsibility do we ultimately accept responsibility for our organizations and the people they serve. We need to understand three things to fully assume this responsibility:

First, we must understand our own power and how to use it. As followers, we have far more power than we usually acknowledge. We must understand the sources of our power, whom we serve, and what tools we have to carry forward the group's mission from our unique vantage point.

Second, we must appreciate the value of leaders and cherish the critical contributions they make to our endeavors. We must understand the forces that chisel away at their creativity, good humor, and resolve. We must learn how to minimize these forces and create a climate in which a leader's strengths are magnified, so a leader can better serve the common purpose.

Third, we must understand the seductiveness and pitfalls of the power of leadership. We are all familiar with Lord Acton's quote: "Power tends to corrupt, and absolute power corrupts absolutely." We are all witnesses to the many examples that support its assertion. Yet we are like the person who has never taken hard drugs: though we can intellectually understand that they are addictive, we cannot appreciate their force. We must learn how to counteract this dark tendency of power.

The changes occurring in the world make it an opportune time to develop new models of followership. In the past, centralized organizations used relatively crude instruments and blunt force to coordinate resources in pursuit of their objectives. If you were building a pyramid, this method of organization worked terrifically. If you were laying a railroad, it also worked well. It even worked for a while if you were building cars on an assembly line. Dominant leaders and compliant followers were able to get the job done. In information age organizations, however, hundreds of decentralized units process and rapidly act on highly varied information within the design and purpose of the organization. This requires an entirely different relationship between leaders and followers.

Additionally, in both the West and the East, a new social contract is being formulated. In the largest organizations, we are no longer guaranteed employment. Our health benefits and retirement plans are being made portable. Leaders and organizations will no longer take care of us. Paternalism is gone. We need to take care of ourselves and each other.

In a deep way this is liberating. A central problem in the leader-follower relationship is its tendency to become a parent-child relationship, a relationship in which the follower is dependent and unable to relate to the leader on an equal footing.

A new model of followership can help us reorient ourselves and our relationships with leaders. I am choosing the image of the "courageous follower" to build a model of followership because courage is so antithetical to the prevailing image of followers and so crucial to balancing the relationship with leaders.

Courageous followership is built on the platform of courageous relationship. The courage to be right, the courage to be wrong, the courage to be different from each other. Each of us sees the world through our own eyes and experiences. Our interpretation of the world thus differs. In relationships, we struggle to maintain the validity of our own interpretation while learning to respect the validity of other interpretations.

The danger in the leader-follower relationship is the assumption that the leader's interpretation must dominate. If this assumption exists on the part of either the leader or the follower, they are both at risk. The leader's openness to diversity, empowering others, breakthrough thinking, and being challenged and learning from followers will drop precipitously. Followers will abandon their unique perspectives and healthy dissension, which are at the heart of the creative process and innovation.

Contemporary leadership texts make compelling arguments for leaders to drive fear out of organizations, to share power, to invite feedback, to encourage participation. The leaders likely to read and respond to these arguments are the ones already open to change. What about those who cannot be their own agents of change, who do not walk the talk? I believe that courageous followers can and must be agents of change for such leaders.

But powerful socialization mechanisms, which served centralized bureaucracies well and taught followers to obediently follow, are still largely in force. The awesome shaping powers of school, organized religion, sports teams, the military, and large corporations are weakening, but still, whatever else they teach, they condition followers to obey. Expulsion for nonconformity is a very real threat. The conditioning begins at an age when children are still utterly dependent on their parents for survival and experience considerable anxiety about the consequences of not obeying. Our institutions play on this anxiety and, wittingly or not, reinforce it until followers often do become the timid creatures we emotionally reject identifying with.

We must examine this programming of the follower's role and envision what the role can become. What are our attitudes toward leaders? Where do our loyalties ultimately lie? What outcomes are worse than expulsion? What power do we have to support leaders who are striving to serve their group? And what obligation and power do we have to change things when higher loyalties are betrayed? How courageous do we dare to be?

We have not had a lot of cultural support for doing this. Our mythology until recently has focused on hero-leaders who perform remarkable feats and successfully challenge villain-leaders. We have lacked common-man, common-woman heroes who stay true to their own lights while helping leaders follow theirs. Supportive "number twos" have not historically attracted much press coverage or six-figure publishing advances. Whistle-blowers have fared considerably less well, their lives often seriously disrupted, with few rallying to their support. It is only very recently that we have begun to see exceptions to this pattern. The time has come for leaders and followers to develop and honor new models for relating to each other.

I will first explore the dynamics of the leader-follower relationship. What binds the leader and follower together? What are the underlying moral, emotional, and psychological forces at work? What are the respective powers each has in the relationship? I will then present a model of how courageous followers can improve that relationship for the benefit of themselves, their leaders, and the organization.

There are four dimensions in which a courageous follower operates within a group, and a fifth dimension in which the follower operates either within or outside the group depending on the response of the leadership. The model will explore each of these dimensions as a way to compare our current followership practices with how we might develop the follower role.

THE FIVE DIMENSIONS OF COURAGEOUS FOLLOWERSHIP

THE COURAGE TO ASSUME RESPONSIBILITY

Courageous followers assume responsibility for themselves and the organization. They do not hold a paternalistic image of the leader or organization; they do not expect the leader or organization to provide for their security and growth, or to give them permission to act. Courageous followers discover or create opportunities to fulfill their potential and maximize their value to the organization. They initiate values-based action to improve the organization's external activities and its internal processes. The "authority" to initiate comes from the courageous follower's understanding and ownership of the common purpose, and from the needs of those the organization serves.

THE COURAGE TO SERVE

Courageous followers are not afraid of the hard work required to serve a leader. They assume new or additional responsibilities to unburden the leader and serve the organization. They stay alert for areas in which their strengths complement the leader's and assert themselves in these areas. Courageous followers stand up for their leader and the tough decisions a leader must make if the organization is to achieve its purpose. They are as passionate as the leader in pursuing the common purpose.

THE COURAGE TO CHALLENGE

Courageous followers give voice to the discomfort they feel when the behaviors or policies of the leader or group conflict with their sense of what is right. They are willing to stand up, to stand out, to risk rejection, to initiate conflict in order to examine the actions of the leader and group when appropriate. They are willing to deal with the emotions their challenge evokes in the leader and group. Courageous followers value organizational harmony and their relationship with the leader, but not at the expense of the common purpose and their integrity.

THE COURAGE TO PARTICIPATE
IN TRANSFORMATION

When behavior that jeopardizes the common purpose remains unchanged, courageous followers recognize the need for transformation. They champion the need for change and stay with the leader and group while they mutually struggle with the difficulty of real change. They examine their own need for transformation and become full participants in the change process as appropriate.

THE COURAGE TO TAKE MORAL ACTION

Courageous followers know when it is time to take a stand that is different from that of the leader's. They are answering to a higher set of values. The stand may involve refusing to obey a direct order, appealing the order to the next level of authority, or tendering one's resignation. These and other forms of moral action involve personal risk. But service to the common purpose justifies and sometimes demands acting. If attempts to redress the morally objectionable situation fail, a follower faces the more difficult prospect of whether to become a whistleblower, with the greatly increased risks this poses to both the follower and the organization.

Enriching the original model are two chapters added in the subsequent editions.

THE COURAGE TO SPEAK TO THE HIERARCHY

The five classes of courageous follower behaviors assume a degree of relationship with the leader. In large hierarchical and global organizations, policies or directives often originate several levels above the follower, from individuals with whom the follower has little or no contact. How do those lower in the hierarchy, or far removed from the formal power centers, effectively communicate with those near the top of the hierarchy? How do they ensure that the most senior leaders of the organization have the data they need to make well-informed decisions? And how do nonhierarchical methods of communication that leverage the power of networks interface with these hierarchies? Courageous followers give careful thought to the application of courageous follower principles in these contexts and develop the sensitivities and strategies required to speak effectively to the hierarchy.

THE COURAGE TO LISTEN TO FOLLOWERS

After exploring the model and applications of courageous followership, I will conclude with an exploration of the leader's responsibility to support the conditions of courageous followership and to respond productively to acts of courageous followership. This is harder to do than it appears to be on the surface. When done well, it offers powerful paybacks for the leader and the organization. When done poorly, both leaders' careers and their organizations suffer.

The world is fitfully evolving to a more egalitarian culture. Leadership and followership are evolving. Leaders are increasingly becoming a hub in a complex system of multiple wheels and hubs and spokes. Dynamic follower-follower relations are becoming as essential as dynamic leader-follower and follower-leader relations. The realities of knowledge-driven organizations require this evolution. Nevertheless, in all evolutionary processes, the prospects for the emerging stage of development often look dubious. There will be times while reading this book when you might wince at suggested behaviors and think, "Get real!" For some leaders the suggested approach will be unreal or at least uncomfortable. For others, who have allowed contemporary cultural changes to seep into their patterning, the approach presented here will be recognizable and welcome. The leader's reactions are of secondary importance, however, to the actions of the follower. That is why this book focuses on the courage of the follower; we are not talking about comfortable, risk-free behavior.

Most of us will have ample opportunity to experiment with and develop new models of courageous followership in the course of "ordinary" living. We will help our organizations compete more efficiently, make them more humane and environmentally thoughtful, help our community groups function more responsively, perhaps even teach our children to be more courageous in relating to legitimate authority figures and illegitimate ones such as schoolyard bullies who, unchecked, grow into workplace or political bullies.

But the extraordinary also occurs: the opportunity to help a leader make a bold peace initiative, the discovery of abusive practices that demand reversal, the chance to influence leadership practices that may bring an organization to a crossroads in choosing the core values by which it will live. To the degree we have become strong and comfortable with new models of followership, those models will serve us well when we find ourselves in situations where the consequences are profound.

Whether we are dealing with the ordinary or extraordinary, the challenge a follower faces is significant. This book is designed to give the courageous follower the insights and tools needed to meet that challenge.

1

THE DYNAMICS OF THE LEADER-FOLLOWER RELATIONSHIP

I USED TO HAVE ASPIRATIONS to work closely with prominent leaders but found that when I was actually with them, I would clutch, become tongue-tied, or engage more in flattery than dialogue. In doing this, I wasted whatever opportunity there may have been to develop a meaningful relationship with the leader in which we learned from each other.

When still in the "aspiring" state, I would look forward to being seated at the same table as the head of the organization at a company banquet. Later, as I discovered my nervousness about the interaction, I purposely avoided this close contact. Yet a colleague of mine, who was affable but not normally ingratiating, always aggressively sat himself next to the president of the company if he could. He was incredulous that others did not fight for the opportunity to bring themselves to the president's attention. For both my colleague and me, the mere fact of close contact with the leader produced changes in how we usually behaved with other people.

As a leader myself, I observed who would influence me and whom I was prone to ignore or dismiss. The people who influenced me from a lateral or subordinate position seemed to have a deep, natural sense of self-worth. They needed this quality because at times I could present a pretty gruff image, which would intimidate a less confident person. They were able to separate out this aspect of my personality and not interpret it as their own failing. They knew their specialties, observed and respected my strengths, supported my efforts, and spoke to me forthrightly when they thought I was off the mark. They also cared as much as I did about the organization's purpose and our success in achieving it.

In this chapter I examine the challenges we face in establishing and maintaining a true relationship with a leader. By "true," I mean a relationship in which we can comfortably meet a leader as one human being to another. In a true relationship, we are neither retiring nor fawning nor manipulative. We work together with mutual respect and honesty to achieve our common purpose.

THE COMMON PURPOSE
AND CORE VALUES

Any organization is a triad consisting of leaders and followers joined in a common purpose. The purpose is the atomic glue that binds us. It gives meaning to our activities.

Followers and leaders both orbit around the purpose; followers do not orbit around the leader.

Often the purpose exists and we come together around it. Sometimes the leader envisions it and draws us to it. At other times we formulate or redefine the purpose together. If the purpose is not clear and motivating, leaders and followers can only pursue their perceived self-interest, not their common interest. The process of clarifying purpose can mobilize a group, heal painful rifts, and help the group steer through treacherous passages. It is a critical act of strong leadership and courageous followership.

Equally fundamental are the group's shared values. Clarifying core values validates the purpose and determines how we will and how we won't pursue it. If the purpose is pursued in the context of decent human values, it serves as a guiding light in navigating our relationship with a leader. If the purpose intrinsically violates or is pursued in a way that violates decent human values, however, it is not an ethically valid guide. For example, "making a profit for shareholders" is a purpose we can use to guide our actions. "Making a profit regardless of the impact on the community or environment" nullifies its validity in determining appropriate action.

A common purpose pursued with decent values is the heart of the healthy leader-follower relationship.

THE PARADOX OF FOLLOWERSHIP

We are responsible. Whether we lead or follow, we are responsible for our own actions, and we share responsibility for the actions of those whom we can influence.

All important social accomplishments require complex group effort and, therefore, leadership and followership. Both are necessary in the pursuit of a common purpose. Some believe that influence in the leader-follower relationship is largely one-way. This is far from true. Followers have great capacity to influence the relationship.

Just as a leader is accountable for the actions and performance of followers, so followers are accountable for their leaders. We must support leaders and, when necessary, help them correct their actions, just as they must support us and help us correct our actions. This is partnership. Both sides must be proactive. If we have followers who are partners with leaders, we will not have leaders who are tyrants.

Leadership may be informal and distributed throughout an organization. But formal leadership, which has final accountability and authority, is usually vested in an elected or appointed or self-proclaimed leader or small group. At the extremes, the formal leaders of a group may be wise or arrogant, servants or parasites, visionaries or demagogues. More commonly, leaders are a rich blend of strengths and weaknesses, of qualities that add and subtract value, and there is the potential for either side of their personalities to grow while in office. The quality and courage of followers influence which of the leader's characteristics will grow.

If we amplify our leaders' strengths and modulate their weaknesses, we are the gem cutters of leadership, coaxing out its full brilliance. If we amplify our leaders' weaknesses, we may stress existing fracture lines in their characters, and these fracture lines may become fatal flaws. Followers who are closest to a leader carry pivotal responsibility; they markedly shape the tone and outcomes of a leader's tenure.

Courageous followership is full of paradox:

> **A courageous follower has a clear internal vision of service while being attracted to a leader who articulates and embodies its external manifestation.**

> **Courageous followers remain fully accountable for their actions while relinquishing some autonomy and conceding certain authority to a leader.**

> **A central dichotomy of courageous followership is the need to energetically perform two opposite roles: implementer and challenger of the leader's ideas.**

> **There is inherent tension between the identity a follower derives from group membership and the individuation required to question and creatively challenge the group and its leadership.**

Followers often benefit from the leader as mentor, learning crucial things, yet at the same time must be willing to teach the leader.

At times, courageous followers need to lead from behind, breathing life into their leader's vision or even vision into the leader's life.

Senior followers often are important leaders in their own right and must integrate within themselves the perspectives of both leadership and followership.

The concept of a "courageous follower" appears to some to be an oxymoron but, if embraced, enables followers to join leaders fully as stewards of the group's trust.

WHO DOES A FOLLOWER SERVE?

Follower is not synonymous with *subordinate*. A subordinate reports to an individual of higher rank and may in practice be a supporter, an antagonist, or indifferent. A follower shares a common purpose with the leader, believes in what the organization is trying to accomplish, wants both the leader and organization to succeed, and works energetically to this end.

Like the leader, the follower is a steward of the resources an organization can draw on to carry out its work. The resources of a group include its leaders. Thus, a follower is a leader's steward every bit as much as a leader is the follower's steward.

We can perform our role as followers at different levels:

At the purest level, we serve those whom the organization exists to serve—its members, clients, constituents, customers, communities—often called stakeholders because of their stake in the outcome of the group's actions.

Below that, and quite functionally, we simultaneously serve the organization's stakeholders, its leaders, and ourselves, with no conflict of interest.

Below that, we serve the leaders and ourselves but not the stake-holders. While we may be rewarded for this in the short run, we sow the seeds of the organization's failure.

At the lowest level, we serve the leaders while permitting them to harm the organization and its stakeholders through corruption, and we participate in that corruption ourselves.

If we serve only ourselves and not the leaders or the stakeholders, we are not followers but opportunists siphoning off the energy of the group to serve our own agendas.

SELF-INTEREST AND COMMON PURPOSE

True leaders and followers are dedicated to the common purpose. At the same time, other than in rare cases of idealism and self-sacrifice, leaders and followers also bring their self-interest to the relationship and their work.

There is nothing inherently problematic about self-interest as long as it does not eclipse the common purpose. There is tremendous energy generated in the pursuit of self-interest. It is energy that if properly aligned brings great value to the organization.

Leaders who remain aware and supportive of the self interest of their followers generate loyalty and commitment. It is similarly valuable for followers to remain aware of the self-interest of leaders. What are their aspirations? What would help a leader realize the aspiration? What would jeopardize the dream?

There are many priorities and voices competing for leaders' attention. To sufficiently interest leaders in adding another item to their overflowing plates, it is sometimes necessary to frame the matter in terms of both purpose and aspirations.

Similarly, while pursuing one's own interests, followers need to stay self-aware that these align with the mission, rather than compete with it. Honest self-appraisal is required for appropriate balance. Be careful here. It is human to rationalize. Courageous followership demands rigorous self-honesty.

We have the right to be advocates for our self-interest within service to the purpose. We can ask for support and, within reason, expect to receive it. We do not have the right to manipulate the leader and group to serve our self-interest at the expense of the common purpose.

LOYALTY OF A FOLLOWER

In the past, when relationships were more stable and lifelong social contracts were the norm, loyalty was unquestioningly given—to the clan, to the feudal lord, to the sole employer. Unquestioning loyalty is, of course, fraught with moral peril. Today, relationships are constantly shifting and loyalty is problematic—who deserves it and why? Yet the lifting of cultural pressure to give blind loyalty allows us the freedom to make conscious moral choices based on our core values.

Placing our loyalty somewhere is an important act of identity. We can place it in ourselves, and often this is important to help us stay a difficult course. But if we place no loyalty outside ourselves, we become a kind of brigand, justifying any action regardless of its cost to others.

Leaders and followers who find themselves in constantly shifting configurations need to find a mutual place for their loyalty that transcends the impermanence of their relationship yet bonds them in a framework of trust. This is the importance of the contemporary emphasis on vision, values, and mission statements: well formulated, these define the loyalty that leaders and followers pledge to those who have a stake in the group.

The values statement evokes a circumscribed loyalty—to fairness, to quality, to honesty, to service, to a common purpose. Circumscribed loyalty to worthy values avoids the pitfalls of unlimited loyalty and may be an evolutionary step forward. Both leaders and followers are entering into a contract to pursue the common purpose within the context of their values. The loyalty of each is to the purpose and to helping each other stay true to that purpose.

If leadership and followership are both forms of stewardship, then loyalty is correctly directed to the organization's purpose and its stakeholders. It appropriately includes and embraces the principles, people, and environments affected by the organization's actions. Once appropriate loyalty is clarified, it can inform our decisions to support or challenge a leader's agenda.

POWER IN THE LEADER-FOLLOWER RELATIONSHIP

Wherever an organization lies on the spectrum from "hierarchical" to "shared" leadership, some power is always vested in the leaders and some in the followers. In shared leadership, the power is more balanced although one faction may accumulate power over other factions. In an autocratic hierarchy, power appears to reside almost entirely with the leader until something occurs that causes the followers to depose the leader and reclaim their power.

The situation in which power appears to reside entirely with the leader is very dangerous both for the follower, who can be ruined at the leader's whim, and for the leader, whose followers become sycophantic. Sycophants act according to what they have learned is expected of them in a situation. They do not observe or think well for themselves, and often fail to take appropriate actions. This hurts the leader and the organization.

As followers, our formal powers are unequal to the leader's, and we must learn to participate effectively in the relationship despite this imbalance. We may have far more power than we imagine, however, and too often fail to exercise the power we do have. It is critical for followers to connect with their power and learn how to use it. To maintain and strengthen power, it must be used; otherwise, it will wither.

The sources of a follower's power are varied:

The power of purpose, the strength that comes from commitment to the common good

The power of knowledge, the possession of skills and resources the organization and its leadership value and do not want to lose

The power of personal history, a record of successes and unassailable contributions to the leader and the organization

The power of faith in self, belief in our observations and intentions, in our integrity and commitment

The power to speak the truth, as we see it, to the leadership

The power to set a standard that influences others, to model values and behavior for the leader and group members

The power to choose how to react in a situation regardless of what is done or threatened by others

The power to follow or not follow in a given direction

The power of relationships, of networks of people who know and trust us

The power to communicate through a variety of channels

The power to organize others of like mind

The power to withdraw support if the leadership's actions violate our values

If we are to be effective partners with leaders, it is important to remember that as followers we possess our own power, quite apart from the reflected power of the leader.

VALUE OF THE FOLLOWER

Follower is not a term of weakness but the condition that permits leadership to exist and gives it strength. Dynamic followers recognize their own aspirations in the leader's vision. They follow their own light, which the leader intensifies. They give 110 percent, not because the leader "motivates them" but because they are inspired—the spirit of the activity is within them. They are interdependent with, not dependent on, the leader. They add value to both themselves and the leader through this relationship.

The value of a follower is measured by how completely the follower helps the leader and organization pursue their common purpose within the context of their values. Certain characteristics help to do this:

Effective followers are cooperative and collaborative, qualities essential to all human progress.

Trusted followers integrate their ego needs sufficiently into their communal responsibilities to serve rather than compete with the leader.

Well-balanced followers are less prone to the pitfalls that await leaders with strong egos and can serve as guides around these pitfalls.

Caring followers perceive the needs of both the leader and other group members and try to form a bridge between them.

We retain our value as followers to the degree we remain true to those whom our organization serves, to the degree we are courageous in doing this. If we bend to the will of a leader when it conflicts with the interests of our stakeholders, or if we bend to the will of our stakeholders when it conflicts with the higher values of humanity, our value is greatly diminished.

COURAGE OF THE FOLLOWER

Courage is the great balancer of power in relationships. An individual who is not afraid to speak and act on the truth as she perceives it, despite external inequities in a relationship, is a force to be reckoned with.

Courage implies risk. If there is no risk, courage is not needed. Life, of course, is full of risk at every turn, at every moment. We usually structure our lives to reduce risk to an acceptable level. Courage requires a willingness to consciously raise our level of risk, at least in the short term.

A priest must be willing to tell the bishop that moral turpitude is being covered up in his see. An aide must be willing to tell the governor that her policies will cause severe hardship. A midlevel manager must be willing to tell senior management that by only paying lip service to quality or customer service they are undermining its implementation.

While silence may appear the safe choice, it often leaves our relationships with leaders or peers sapped of the vitality that honest dialogue produces. A follower needs the courage of an inquisitive child who asks questions without fear, but also needs the courage of an adult who bears the responsibility for a family. The family's need for security may clash with the need to risk that security for higher principles. This is a core issue, for without the willingness to risk on this profound level, we won't speak the truth. From where can we draw the courage to speak and act our truth and not be inhibited from doing so by the potential consequences?

On a practical level, if our livelihood depends on our position with the leader, it is healthy for us to develop contingency plans should we fall out of favor. Another job opportunity, money in the bank to support us for a year, a working spouse or partner—any of these can provide a safety net that makes our leap of courage less intimidating. If our career will be jeopardized by a clash with the leader, plotting alternate career paths can reduce the potential severity of the consequences. Being prepared to be fired or blackballed in our industry is the antidote to silencing ourselves.

On a deeper level, each of us may find our own courage springs from a different source:

Our religious beliefs

Our philosophy

A role model

A vision of the future

A vow made from past experience

An event that tested us

A conviction we hold

Our values

Our empathy for others

Our self-esteem

Commitment to our comrades

Outrage felt toward injustice

If we are clear on the source of our courage, it prepares us to accept the consequences of our actions. To act courageously, we may not need to free ourselves from fear but to experience our fear in the context of our source of courage. If you have ever been in a situation you believed was truly dangerous, you know the intensity of the emotional energy generated by fear. Suppressing the energy contained in this fear and "rising above it" is one strategy. Another strategy, perhaps more effective, is to let the fear rise up fully, acknowledge it, and then channel the energy locked within that fear into the service of our principles and goals. If our principles and goals are clear, enormous self-empowerment can occur.

We probably have to fail a few times before we succeed. The first time we are confronted with the use of raw power, with its assumptions and attitude and force, it is so startling that we may well flinch or freeze. We may need to go away and prepare ourselves to meet it again.

Our "courage muscle" will develop to the degree we exercise it. If we exercise it when the risks are small, it will be strong enough to meet the challenge when the risks are large. Ultimately, there are no formulas for courage: we develop it through determination and practice, self-forgiveness when we fail, and growth when we learn.

BALANCE THROUGH RELATIONSHIP

In different situations, different qualities are most needed and productive—courage, diplomacy, consistency, firmness—all are virtues that have their place. But any virtue taken to an extreme and used in the wrong situation can become a vice: courage becomes recklessness, diplomacy becomes appeasement, consistency becomes rigidity, firmness becomes brutality.

As a leader acquires power, qualities that contribute to success are affirmed and reinforced and may begin to be relied on excessively. When a leader receives only positive feedback, these qualities can be reinforced to the point where they become dysfunctional. Similarly, flaws that may be of minor consequence when power is small can become magnified with the increase of power. In either case, the leader's talents may be eclipsed by weaknesses.

Dynamic leaders are the spark, the flame that ignites action. With vision, they generate and focus power. But followers are the guarantors of the beneficial use of that power. Dynamic leaders may use power well, but they cannot be the guarantors. In their passion, their expansiveness, their drive, dynamic leaders are prone to excess: a deal too large, a bottom line too important, a cause too righteous, an image too pure, a lifestyle too rich, an enemy too hated, a bridge too far. We provide the balance *if* we can stand up to our leaders.

At the heart of balance is the dual nature of the universe—I and the other—and the necessity for relationship. Genuine relationships will not tolerate extremes, which become abusive. The key to personal balance for leaders is the quality of their relationships with followers. Honest, open relationships will provide a steady stream of uncensored feedback. It is only through this feedback that leaders can accurately perceive and modulate their behavior, policies, and strategies.

Because of the unknowns, it takes courage for us to be open and direct with a leader while building a relationship.

How open is this leader willing to be with anyone?

How open can I be about myself?

Do I know how to read this person yet?

How does this individual respond to feedback?

If an issue is emotionally laden for me, how do I know my concern isn't exaggerated, or that I'll present it well?

As I am rewarded for serving a leader well, how do I make sure I don't begin seeing the leader through self-serving lenses?

If we are not willing to risk whatever relationship we have built with a leader by providing honest feedback, we instead risk losing the whole dream for which we have both been working. We will grow more cynical about the leader, and the leader will grow increasingly unreal about the impact of his actions. Two essential elements of relationship are developing trust and then using that trust to speak honestly when appropriate; one without the other is meaningless. The challenge for the courageous follower is to maintain a genuine relationship with the leader, not the pseudorelationship of the sycophant.

MATURE RELATIONSHIPS

Oddly enough, one of the challenges followers often face is helping leaders develop tolerance, decency, and, in a sense, maturity. All humans struggle with the need to grow up, to accept that the rest of the world is not here to serve us, that people are going to differ with us, and that this is okay. The world soon teaches most of us these lessons, and we find ways of coping with our younger egocentric view of life even if we do not fully transform it.

When skill and circumstances combine to put us in a position of formal leadership, our early egocentric impulses are vulnerable to reemergence. If, as too often happens, leaders are surrounded by followers who kowtow to them, the immature parts of their personality, which have not been fully transformed, tend to regain dominance.

If the immature aspects of a leader's personality appear with increased frequency, this leaves us in the odd and difficult position of serving a leader who is competent, even brilliant in some dimensions, and a spoiled brat in other respects. The internal confusion and conflict that a follower may feel when confronted by the discrepancy between the mature and immature traits of a leader should not be underestimated: is this brilliant, sometimes abusive leader deserving of my support or not?

This would not be such a difficult question if we felt empowered to challenge a leader about the immature behavior while supporting the mature skills and judgment he brings to the group. If our behavior is disruptive to the group, the leader is expected to raise the issue with us; similarly, we need to break the taboo against our raising behavior issues with the leader.

It is difficult to break the taboo because our early conditioning about leaders takes place in childhood, at home and school, where others are held responsible for our behavior but we are not held responsible for theirs. The power of our early conditioning is so strong that for most of us it is an act of courage to confront a leader about counterproductive behavior, instead of an ordinary act of relationship.

As in so many aspects of relationship, if we have difficulty with a leader who displays immaturity, it is because we also have issues with maturity. Too often, because of our sense of powerlessness, we complain protractedly to others about a leader's behavior instead of taking effective action.

We do not serve the leader or organization well by immaturely whining about a leader's behavior instead of confronting the leader and participating in a process of mutual development.

It requires a courageous follower to confront a powerful leader about immature behavior. The situation can resemble confronting a young child holding a loaded gun: you may be shot persuading the child to put it down. It requires a skillful follower to confront a leader in a way that simultaneously respects the accomplished adult, preserves the adult's self-esteem, and challenges the immature behavior.

DIFFERENCES IN ELEVATION

Overcoming the sometimes very large differences in position within an organization can be a challenge in establishing a true relationship with a leader. Though we may work closely with the leader, the difference in the relative status or elevation of our positions can form a chasm in the relationship. The sources of an elevation gap are varied:

The leader has been elected, and the follower has been hired.

The leader founded the organization.

The leader owns the company.

The leader is considerably older and has held many elevated positions.

The leader holds a formal senior rank.

The leader is wealthy.

The leader has made major contributions to the organization.

The leader is widely regarded as a genius, a hero, or a celebrity.

These conditions may prompt us to think, "Who am I to question this person?" and disregard our perceptions or interpretations of events. We must stay highly alert to this reflex reaction and question it carefully. If it is the premise of our relationship, we will fail both ourselves and the leader.

Warren Bennis, the great student and teacher of leadership, reports that 70 percent of followers will not question a leader's point of view even when they feel the leader is about to make a mistake. From their elevated positions, leaders are prone to losing touch with the common reality. This is sometimes referred to as "the king's disease." Leaders are often dependent on the perceptions of followers to reconnect them to external realities.

If we have thoughtfully considered the merits of our observations, our challenge is to rise above the intimidating nature of the difference in elevation and present our ideas. Speaking forthrightly to an "elevated" leader is not presumptuous; it is an essential part of courageous followership.

FINDING EQUAL FOOTING WITH THE LEADER

To look a leader in the eye and credibly deliver unpalatable observations or sharply differing opinions requires an internal sense of equal worth. Metaphorically, a pygmy cannot look a giant in the eye. Followers usually cannot match up to a leader's external qualities, such as the trappings of formal power, and must find their equal footing on intellectual, moral, or spiritual ground. How can we do this?

If we remember and speak to our common humanity, we need not be seduced, dazzled, or intimidated by the symbols of higher office. Neither we nor the leaders we support are our titles, whether this be secretary, boss, president, or emperor. We are human beings who pass through this existence with gifts and needs, anxieties and dreams, strengths and vulnerabilities. If we, as leaders and followers, remember our common nature, we will deal with each other out of mutual respect, not out of disdain or awe.

We need to closely observe ourselves in the presence of power to see how we behave. If we find ourselves speaking or acting with exaggerated deference, we are relating to the title, not to the person carrying it. If we observe ourselves being even subtly obsequious toward a leader, we should try to look past the title, trappings, and power of office to see the human being occupying the office. Who is the leader outside this specific role?

Where has he come from?

What are his values?

Does his private persona differ from his professional one?

Does he feel supported or lonely?

Is he genuinely confident or perhaps masking insecurity?

Can he be playful?

Does he have a sense of serving a higher ideal or power?

Can we envision him as a parent, a son, a husband?

What failures and tragedies has he experienced?

What are his fears?

What are his aspirations?

Depending on how private the leader is, we may not be able to answer all these questions. And the answers are not as important as our ability to touch the leader's humanity. We need to demythologize leaders, to see them holistically, to be able to identify with their pain and joy so we can talk to them as one human being to another. We need to be able to comfortably ask ourselves, "How can I help this fellow human being whose lot has been cast together with mine?" As we answer this, we affirm the worth we bring to the relationship and find our equal footing.

WHEN THE LEADER ISN'T AN EQUAL

A different challenge exists when a leader isn't as qualified for the role as a follower or, in a sense, isn't the follower's equal. There are many circumstances in which this can occur:

Organizational politics

Discrimination

Diversity values and policies

Rotational assignments

Seniority promotion

Family ownership

Election

Appointment

High public profile

Connections

Amiability and charm

When the most capable person is not the leader, a courageous follower faces several challenges. Most important is to deal with our own feelings about the matter. We often find it difficult to work for someone who is slower than we are, who fails to fully and rapidly grasp situations confronting the organization. Rather than feeling intimidated by their position, we may have difficulty masking our disdain. There may be bitterness if we hoped for the number one position ourselves.

We may also find ourselves in situations in which we must decide whether to cover for the leader or to publicly let the leader appear unprepared and unknowledgeable. We may experience ego-based conflict or ethical confusion about this.

Our workload often increases if the leader falls short of the role. Not only do we assume parts of what should be the leader's role, but we also spend extra time educating the leader through memos and briefings. We usually do this for a lot less money and recognition than the leader is receiving. Our resentment can run high.

As difficult as it may be in this situation, our guiding principle should remain service to the organization. It is important to acknowledge our feelings and frustrations, but if we are committed to the common purpose, we will keep working with our leader for its accomplishment. We will use our talent and competencies to help the leader grow and succeed. As long as the leader is giving his best energy to the role, he deserves our private and public support. And it's surprising how much we can learn from even the leaders who don't excel.

Sometimes it is simply that a capable person is given a job for which he has little experience. A newly elected legislator may have a great vision but be an ingenue on how to craft passable legislation. A seasoned aide may need to guide the legislator through the nuances of the issues and politics and the labyrinths of the policy-making process. Eventually, the legislator will master the subject and the process.

The mark of a great leader is the development and growth of followers. The mark of a great follower is the growth of leaders.

TRUST

Leadership surveys show that trust is the single most important factor on which followers evaluate a leader. The reverse is equally true although the word *reliability* is often substituted when speaking of followers. Reliability is a composite of trust and competence, and a leader needs to experience both in a follower. Competence itself, while valued, can be threatening if the leader senses that the follower is motivated more by a personal agenda than by a desire to support the leader and group.

Trust is essential in the leader-follower relationship if followers are to serve and influence the leader and organization. Yet sometimes it is elusive. How is trust won?

> Trust is a subtle state between two people formed from an assessment of each other's internal motives and external actions—if either are questionable trust does not gel.

> The gelling agents of trust are our word and the judgment and effectiveness we display in our actions.

> To earn trust we must go to great lengths to keep our word, and, if we cannot keep it, we must communicate this as soon as possible.

> To maintain trust we must listen carefully to both external signals and our inner voice, which quietly warn us against actions that may be in poor judgment.

> To enhance trust we must understand the outcomes needed by the leader and group, and overcome the obstacles to those outcomes without violating our core values.

Trust is a quality of relationship that can quickly return to its fluid, uncertain state in response to events and perceptions. Often we sense the change in trust before anything specific has been said or done about it, much as we sense an oncoming storm. If we sense a weakening of trust, we should make aggressive efforts to find out why, as it is the foundation of our relationship. It may be that we appear to have violated trust when we have not. In this case we should take great pains to clarify the situation, using any available documentation to dispel doubt.

If we have, indeed, violated trust through poor judgment or otherwise, the instinct to rationalize it can deliver a death knell to the relationship. Only by genuinely accepting responsibility for our actions and doing what we can to alleviate their consequences can we begin repairing trust.

If we have given genuine cause for trust to be lowered, it may dismay us to find how much time and contribution to the group is required before the breech is healed. A strong commitment to achieving the common purpose will be needed to sustain us through a difficult period.

FOLLOWERS AS LEADERS

In different situations, at different times, we are all followers or leaders. The best way to learn to lead is to work closely with a capable leader. But whether or not the leader is a positive role model, to the degree we are courageous followers we prepare ourselves to be courageous leaders.

Even as we follow, we often are simultaneously expected to lead others in a chain of authority. The dual role of follower and leader gives us ample opportunity to learn to perform better in both roles. It is an art to move fluidly between these roles and remain consistent in our treatment of others.

> **By staying aware of our reactions to those we follow, we learn to be more sensitive to our effect on those we lead.**

> **By staying aware of our reactions to those we lead, we learn to be more sensitive in our efforts to support those we follow.**

By modeling good leadership with our own followers, we can often influence our leaders. They observe us in our roles and borrow from our successes as we do from theirs. If we cannot influence our leader, we can transform even a miserable relationship into a rich learning opportunity if we use it to learn what demotivates followers and commit to not repeating these mistakes ourselves.

To effectively support a leader, we often need to create our own support, our own group to execute that part of the mission with which we are entrusted. There is a danger we will be perceived as empire building if the team we create is especially strong. While leaders value our creating top-notch operations, they may also feel threatened by it. Our intention is of the essence. If we are genuinely serving the organization and its stakeholders, we won't use our strength to thwart the leader's initiatives or jockey for the leader's position. Our team will know they serve the common purpose, not us.

In the dance of leaders and followers, we change partners and roles throughout our lives. With each new partner we must subtly adjust our movements and avoid the other's toes. If we are leading, we must lead; and if we are not, we must follow, but always as a strong partner. We constantly learn from each other and improve our gracefulness in a wide diversity of styles and tempos.

WORKING WITH OTHER FOLLOWERS

While examining the leader-follower relationship, it is important to bear in mind that the dynamics are much more complex than those between two individuals. There are usually at least several followers who are close to the leader, and the interaction between followers profoundly affects the group. Trust between the members of this group is as critical as trust between a leader and follower.

As in a family, there are issues of alliances and shifting alliances, favoritism and perceived favoritism, treatment according to birth order and gender, competing needs and demands for attention, differing styles and invidious comparisons, and limited resources. If these issues can be managed, the group will find strength in both diversity and unity.

There are at least two broad dimensions in these group relationships that courageous followers must stay alert to—how followers relate to each other and how they relate collectively to the leader.

How followers relate to each other:

Staying alert to the individual needs of each member brings us into collaborative unity rather than fractious competitiveness.

Appreciating our differences enables us to utilize those differences in the service of the common purpose.

Respecting each other's boundaries allows us to cross them by mutual consent without triggering turf warfare.

Building strong lateral communication and coordination among ourselves enables us to accomplish our functions.

Participating in creative thinking about issues instead of rigidly defending our positions invites the power of synergy into the group.

Remembering whom we serve will help us find common ground when we seem to be splitting into factions.

If we need to compete, it is best to outdo each other in forwarding the common purpose rather than in undermining each others' efforts.

Being willing to both lead and follow our peers, as the situation warrants, permits competency-based leadership.

How followers relate to the leader:

A follower's need to shine for the leader at the expense of the other stars in the group will cause stellar explosions in the group dynamics.

When presenting our counsel to the leader, we will earn both our peers' and the leader's trust if we also present full and fair descriptions of our peers' positions.

When followers bring their internal squabbles to the leader, it drains the leader and evokes impatient and poorly thought-out responses.

If a leader plays one follower against another, we need to resist the attractiveness of temporarily being in favor, and work collectively to change the dynamic.

When our peers act courageously toward the leader, it is critical that we support them and do not leave them out on the proverbial limb alone.

An effective follower stays sensitive to the complex dynamics within the leader's close support group. The dance has now become a lively reel, and we pay attention to all the whirling partners continuously changing positions within the dance's framework.

2

THE COURAGE
TO ASSUME
RESPONSIBILITY

THE MOST FREQUENT COMPLAINT I hear from leaders is that they would like the members of their team to assume more responsibility for the organization and initiate ideas and action on their own. While there are often very good reasons team members don't do this, embedded in either the leader's style or the organizational culture, it is interesting to hear that most leaders want their staff to take more initiative. They don't want to be the only one leading. Recent research on courageous follower behaviors shows that, although each of the behaviors is valued, the courage to assume responsibility is as valued by leaders as the other four behaviors in the model combined. Examining our preparedness to exercise this responsibility is a crucial platform for moving toward partnership with a leader.

When I was at the University of California at Berkeley in the early sixties, a confrontation between the police and students erupted over the subject of free speech. The confrontation happened in the student plaza while the ad hoc student leadership and the administration negotiated the issues elsewhere. I was one of the hundreds of followers supporting the student leadership. By nightfall hundreds of police and thousands of students on both sides of the issue had amassed. The atmosphere was growing ugly, with stink bombs and epithets being hurled at the demonstrators. It looked like the helmeted police would charge into the demonstrators to break up the sit-in. The crowd included a person who was blind and children. I was concerned that people would be hurt.

Joan Baez, the folk singer and political activist, was performing at the Greek theater on another part of the campus that evening. She had recently achieved national fame. I called the hotel where celebrities stay in Berkeley and left her a message describing the situation. I asked her to come to the site of the confrontation, expressing the hope that by having a prominent figure present more restraint would be exercised and violence could be prevented. Though she didn't know me, she responded and appeared a little while later. While she made her presence known, each side restrained itself until a settlement was reached and everyone voluntarily dispersed. I learned the power of taking initiative without formal authority.

Unfortunately, I have not always assumed that much responsibility. Recently, I found myself disappointed by the quality of meetings my company held. The meetings consumed a lot of expense and time as people came from two continents, yet they seemed to cover the same ground each year in an uninspiring format. I complained about it to the organization's founder and president but did nothing else to change it.

Then I had the opportunity to use a self-assessment instrument and was startled to find how disaffected I had become with the president. This flew in the face of my self-image as a positive, contributing team member. I was challenged to assume responsibility for the situation rather than complain while it deteriorated.

I drafted a memo to the other participants in the company meetings and told the president that I intended faxing it to each of them. He supported the initiative. The memo explained what a terrific opportunity I saw in our annual meetings and offered a creative idea for taking better advantage of the meetings. I asked for their feedback. Nearly all replied, several with ideas of their own that I felt improved on mine. Out of this process, and to the president's delight, we constructed a new, stimulating, and valuable format for part of the meeting.

By assuming responsibility for our organization and its activities, we can develop a true partnership with our leader and sense of community with our group. This is how we maximize our own contribution to the common purpose. Assuming responsibility requires courage because we then become responsible for the outcomes—we can't lay the blame for our action or inaction elsewhere.

But before we can assume responsibility for the organization, we must assume responsibility for ourselves. I had to recognize my disaffection and do something to change it. I had to assume responsibility for my own growth. We cannot remain static ourselves and expect to improve the organization.

In this chapter, I explore the responsibility a courageous follower takes for self-development and for the development of the organization. Though we coordinate our activities as appropriate, we also take actions independently of the leader to forward our common purpose.

SELF-ASSESSMENT

Assuming responsibility for our personal development begins with self-examination. We cannot know in which direction we need to grow until we first know where we are. Courageous followers do not wait for performance reviews (strained events that these usually are anyway); they assess their own performance.

In addition to evaluating their job "competencies," courageous followers also examine the more illusive subject of their relationships with teammates and leaders. If charity begins at home, development in the relationship between followers and leaders begins in a follower's vestibule; a follower's issues with authority are the other side of a leader's issues with power.

Our relationship to authority is so deeply ingrained that it is difficult to be fully aware of our beliefs and postures vis-à-vis leaders. For our entire childhoods, at home and school, those in authority had tremendous power to dictate to us. We learned to survive by complying with, avoiding, or resisting those authorities. The strategies we adopted became patterns for future behavior and influence our attitudes toward our current leaders.

Most work environments in adulthood reinforce our childhood relationship to authority. We must strive for greater awareness of our own beliefs, attitudes, and patterns of behavior toward authority, and look at their consequences. For example:

> **Challenging a specific leader on a specific subject may be healthy, but a pattern of challenging all leaders on all subjects is not. A rebellious, alienated follower will never earn the trust to meaningfully influence a leader.**

> A follower's deferential language and demeanor toward a leader
> may be appropriate, but strained subservience or chronic resent-
> ment are not. A follower who is too subservient and eager to
> please authority cannot provide the balance a leader requires to
> use power well.

> Clamming up when a leader interrupts us in a raised voice may
> have been necessary at home or school, but it serves us and the
> leader poorly now. Tolerating disrespect for our voice and views
> will reinforce the behavior and weaken the relationship.

It is important to move beyond viewing a leader as a good parent or
bad parent, a good king or bad king, a hero or villain in our world. If we
become aware of such attitudes, our challenge is to learn to relate to
the leader on a different basis. By paying attention to how we interpret
the leader's actions, to the feelings that interpretation evokes in us, and
to the behaviors we employ to cope with those feelings, we can loosen
our grasp on the mechanisms we once needed for survival. We can begin
to examine what other choices we have as adults for relating effectively
to authority.

FOLLOWERSHIP STYLE

There are different ways to represent our individual style of relating to
leaders. Useful models for doing this can be found in the works by Robert
Kelley and Gene Boccialetti, cited in the bibliography. In my workshops,
I use a two-axis representation derived from the core of the Courageous
Follower model that participants in workshops find helpful in under-
standing their strengths and potential growth needs

The two critical dimensions of courageous followership are the degree
of support a follower gives a leader and the degree to which the follower
is willing to challenge the leader's behavior or policies if these are endan-
gering the organization's purpose or undermining its values. This holds
true at all levels of leadership and followership. We will examine both of
these dimensions in depth in subsequent chapters. At this point, however,
it is useful to reflect on where you place yourself in this matrix of follower
behaviors.

The possible combinations of these two dimensions produce four quadrants that can depict the posture you tend to assume in relation to leaders. There is variance, of course, depending on the leader to whom you are relating. But, if you change quadrants radically based on the leader's temperament and style, you are ceding too much power to the leader to determine your professional behavior. It is useful to identify your core tendency or natural position in relationship to authority at this point in your personal development. Then you can chart a growth path for yourself.

The four possible quadrants in this model of followership style are these:

Quadrant I: high support, high challenge

Quadrant II: high support, low challenge

Quadrant III: low support, high challenge

Quadrant IV: low support, low challenge

High Support

QUADRANT II IMPLEMENTER	QUADRANT I PARTNER
QUADRANT IV RESOURCE	QUADRANT III INDIVIDUALIST

Low
Challenge

High
Challenge

Low Support

QUADRANT I: HIGH SUPPORT,
HIGH CHALLENGE—THE PARTNER

A follower operating from the first quadrant gives vigorous support to a leader but is also willing to question the leader's behavior or policies. This individual could be said to be a true partner with the leader and displays many of the characteristics identified with courageous followership in this book. Even within this quadrant, of course, there is room for growth as one can become stronger and more skillful in both dimensions.

QUADRANT II: HIGH SUPPORT, LOW CHALLENGE—THE IMPLEMENTER

This is the quadrant from which most leaders love to have their followers operate. Leaders can count heavily on followers who operate from this profile to do what is needed to get the job done and not require much oversight or explanation. However, if the leader begins to go down a wrong path, these are not the followers who are likely to tell the leader so, or, if they do, they are not likely to pursue the matter if the leader rebuffs their attempts. Growth for those tending to this style of followership lies in the direction of being more willing to challenge a leader's problematic actions or policies and learning to do so effectively and productively.

QUADRANT III: LOW SUPPORT, HIGH CHALLENGE—THE INDIVIDUALIST

Surrounding every leader are one or two individuals whose deference is quite low and who do not hesitate to tell the leader, or anyone else in the group, exactly what they think of his or her actions or policies. These are potentially important people to have in the group as they balance the tendency of the rest of the group to go along with what seems acceptable while harboring reservations. However, because these individuals do not display equal energy in supporting the leader's initiatives, they marginalize themselves. Their criticism becomes predictable and tiresome, and the leader finds ways to shut them out. Growth for individuals who operate from this style of followership lies in the direction of increasing their actual and visible support for the leader's initiatives that forward the common purpose.

QUADRANT IV: LOW SUPPORT, LOW CHALLENGE—THE RESOURCE

Any group has a certain number of people who do an honest day's work for a day's pay but don't go beyond the minimum expected of them. There are often legitimate reasons for this. They may be single parents whose

priority is leaving at 3:30 to pick up their children from day care, gradu-
ate students whose priority is excelling in their course work, or volunteers
who can give only a few hours a week. However, it is difficult to advance
their careers or make significant contributions to the organization while
operating from this quadrant. When they are ready to give more priority
to their participation in the group or organization, they must begin to raise
their level of support for the leader and begin to earn the standing to also
credibly challenge policies and behavior.

The following is a summary of the attitudes and behaviors likely to be
displayed by individuals relating to leaders from each of these quadrants.

FOLLOWER STYLES

Implementer	Partner
Dependable	Purpose driven
Supportive	Mission oriented
Considerate	Risk taker
Advocate	Cultivates relationships
Defender	Holds self and others accountable
Team oriented	Confronts sensitive issues
Compliant	Focuses on strengths and growth
Respectful of authority	Peer relations with authority
Reinforces leader's perspectives	Complements leader's perspectives

Resource	Individualist
Present	Confrontational
Available	Forthright
Extra pair of hands	Self-assured
Brings specific skills	Independent thinker
Uncommitted	Reality checker
Primary interests lie elsewhere	Irreverent
Executes minimum requirements	Rebellious
Makes complaints to third parties	Self-marginalizing
Avoids the attention of authority	Unintimidated by authority

While these tendencies can be measured, you probably already have a
sense of how you tend to operate, at least in relationship to the current

leaders with whom you interact. As you read further, keep in mind this self-assessment and the direction in which you feel you would like to grow. You can then consider and test the ideas and suggestions you will encounter to help you do so.

ELICITING FEEDBACK

Although self-assessment is important, finding out how others see us is equally vital. Courageous followers overcome their reticence to hear "criticism"; they learn to encourage honest feedback. Though we have experiences or images of "bosses" giving us streams of criticism about specific tasks, in fact, many do not provide feedback on the more fundamental issues they may have with us. They find it too uncomfortable to do so. They, too, can lack courage in relationships, despite their positional superiority.

Courageous followers draw the leader out despite discomfort on either of their parts:

> "We've been working together for six months. What feedback can you give me about my performance and work style?"

> "Nobody does everything perfectly. What should I work on so I can do the job better?"

If we receive negative feedback, however tenuous, we should encourage it with statements like this:

> "That's useful for me to know—can you tell me more about that?"

This emboldens the leader, who may be testing the water to see if we really do want to hear this. Once a spirit of open communication is established, a courageous follower probes further:

> "Are you concerned about any other aspects of my performance, which may be even more fundamental?"

If we can remain interested and avoid becoming defensive, we can learn crucial things about ourselves and the leader. We should ask for clarification and examples until we are very clear about what change would be desirable.

If the feedback we receive is about an issue on which the leader or others have previously confronted us, hearing further feedback on the subject may raise our understanding of the need to address it and strengthen our resolve to do so. By eliciting feedback we make sure that we, not others, hear about our perceived flaws and that we are in a strong position to consider what to do about them.

PERSONAL GROWTH

Self-assessment and feedback help us determine in what ways it would be desirable for us to change, to grow. Growth requires courage; it is a continuous process of exposing our vulnerable areas, areas where we have not developed mastery. Growth also requires exploring what the Jungians call our "dark" side. This is uncomfortable to do. Yet the courage to assume responsibility includes responsibility for the parts of us that we'd rather not have the world look at too closely. If we are to contain or transform our leader's dark side, we had better become familiar with our own. We must learn to support our urge toward growth in its contest with the equally powerful urge to protect our self-image.

Personal growth often involves emotional struggle. We should be prepared for that struggle and not try to shut it down at the first signs of discomfort. The knowledge that we may feel worse before we feel better is important and enables us to stick with the lessons we need to learn. Supportive relationships or groups help us get through periods of emotional trial. Structured development programs, counseling, and mentor relationships all provide vehicles and support systems for internal growth.

We also need external growth opportunities. There is often ample room for growth within our current position if we assertively seek it. Working closely with a competent leader is itself a primary growth opportunity. At some point, however, it may be desirable to move away from the comfort of our current role to test ourselves in a new, unproven role. In an age when organizations no longer make lifelong commitments to employees, we must chart our own career growth.

Even if we appear to be staying in place in our current position, the way we perform that position requires continuous growth. There are few jobs in the world today that have not been significantly, if not radically, transformed by the impact of technology, communications, and globalization. It is not just that we must learn new technical procedures. In many cases we must change the very way we conceive of our role and how it interfaces with the overlapping roles of others, far and near. On an even deeper level, our sense of professional identity itself may require reexamination. The value we brought in the past may now be widely distributed, demanding that we discover and grow into new ways of providing value.

  ⅄ If we shy away from discomfort, we will never grow. ⅄

  ⅄ If we seek challenge, we will continuously grow, often in unexpected ways. ⅄

Once again, we are responsible. We must be self-advocates for both our internal and external growth.

SELF-MANAGEMENT

We are also responsible for self-management. Our success at self-management creates both the credibility and resources to initiate changes that will improve the organization.

A key to self-management is personal organization. A follower who is not well organized will too often be unprepared, miss deadlines, submit faulty work, or otherwise fail to meet the leader's expectations. If a leader is frustrated with a follower's performance, it is difficult to remain open to the follower's advice and consultation.

Senior followers often lead others. If senior followers lack strong organizational skills, this deficit affects the performance of their teams. If a team struggles to meet even their minimum responsibilities, they will certainly not have the energy to engage in new, creative initiatives.

Self-management encompasses the nuts and bolts of effective leadership or followership. It is mundane. It is pedestrian. Yet self-management is a critical skill, and a courageous follower must be prepared to do the hard work involved in being personally well organized.

We must strive for a high degree of self-organization in several areas:

The way information, requests, and responses flow in and out of our work environment must be clearly established and maintained.

The tools, materials, and information needed to perform a function must be easily accessible and well maintained.

Procedures must be in place to ensure the appropriate safeguarding of information and material.

The criteria and measurements by which work will be judged need to be clearly understood and monitored.

Complex activities should be analyzed and arranged to minimize redundancies and maximize utilization of resources.

Work needs to be scheduled to manage the competing demands on our own and others' time, and the schedule respected.

Requests for service or action should be recorded and trackable to allow for follow-through and timely closure.

Work should be appropriately delegated and delagatees developed and trusted so we do not become a bottleneck in the organization's processes.

If we are not naturally strong in these areas, we must assume responsibility for improving our skills. The most common stumbling block is the feeling we do not have time to get ourselves better organized. Yet often it is the lack of organization that is eating up our time. We must give self-organization attention now, not at some elusive point in the future. We must take time out to sharpen the ax or we'll exhaust ourselves trying to fell trees with a blunt instrument.

Courageous followers will work long and hard to forward the common purpose when necessary, but they also need to organize their work so the output is timely and the pace is sustainable.

TAKING CARE OF OURSELVES

Management of our life and health are even more fundamental than management of our work if we are to be reliable team members and a source of support for our leaders. The more passionately we feel about a leader or cause, the more we are at risk of not taking care of ourselves, sacrificing our health, or damaging our personal relations. There is always another urgent matter to attend to, something that will make a difference.

We must do our jobs, not become our jobs. A follower may feel heroic working fifteen-hour days or ninety-hour weeks. Sometimes we feel pressured into long hours by the example the leader is setting. Occasionally, we do need to work this hard for short periods of time. But if excessive time at work becomes a long-standing pattern, we must change it before it depletes our energy and wreaks havoc in other parts of our lives.

If we do not assume responsibility for getting the nurturing we need as human beings, we will burn out sooner or later. In doing so, we often let down the people we are serving, sometimes very unpleasantly. To serve well we must be passionately committed to our jobs, but not be consumed by that passion.

Ideally, we will find the right balance between work and other parts of our lives. Sometimes we don't manage to do this. We begin to burn out. There are telltale signs: exhaustion, chronic frustration, shortness of temper, frayed relations, feelings of emptiness, lack of caring, wanting to be elsewhere.

We need to stay alert to these signs and periodically examine the balance we are striking:

What areas of our life need attention?

What must be changed to allow us to give that attention?

Are negotiations with the leader needed to make these changes?

Is the relationship with the leader healthy enough to comfortably conduct these negotiations?

Does the leader-follower relationship itself need to be renegotiated?

What are the respective needs that must be balanced for the negotiations to be successful?

Managing our life and health is not a marginal issue. In the long run, it can make the difference between brilliantly contributing to the common purpose and blowing up or fizzling out in the attempt.

PASSION

Successful followers care passionately about their work and the people it serves. They have a sense of ownership, of stewardship. If something happens, it is happening to that for which they are responsible. When followers and leaders share a passion for the work, they can be full partners in it. Unless we match a leader's passion, it is difficult to become more than a junior partner.

We can be passionate for the overall work and also for whatever role we have within it. When the clerk in charge of a supply room or publications stock maintains a beautifully organized facility that smoothly supports the rest of the organization, professional pride shines through. Appreciating the uniqueness of a role and its impact permits us to imbue the role with the energy needed to multiply our contribution.

Passion cannot be manufactured or faked. It springs from genuine connection to the common purpose. It may be clouded by setbacks to that purpose but is always available to be retapped. Courageous followers are not content to accept a loss of passion as "normal." They ask themselves and others tough questions that can reignite passion:

Does the organization's sense of purpose need renewing?

Have I personally lost touch with the shared purpose and vision of the organization?

What is my own vision of fulfillment?

How does my current role allow me to achieve this?

How does my current role position me to achieve even greater fulfillment in the future?

Are frustrations in accomplishing my current role blocking my passion?

Are relationship issues with the leader or other group members diminishing my passion?

Am I ready for more responsibility, and do I need to make this readiness known?

Restoring passion reconnects us with our power. Without passion, we cannot excel. By excelling, we fulfill ourselves and earn the right to help shape the organization's future. Armchair critics have little influence with the leader and group whereas team members passionately fulfilling their role can weigh in heavily.

INITIATIVE

Willingness to initiate action without being instructed to do so is a distinguishing characteristic of the courageous follower. Courageous followers assume responsibility for events in their vicinity—whether it be a customer service complaint or an opportunity that, if seized, can produce a quantum leap forward for the organization.

If we are to strengthen our capacity to initiate, it may help to bear in mind these factors:

> As courageous followers, we view ourselves as full participants committed to shared values and a common purpose. We are not spectators; we don't just watch—we act.

> When a common purpose guides both the leader and follower, control shifts from the leader to the purpose itself; we don't require permission to act in ways that forward the purpose.

> If we understand the organization's purpose, we can initiate fresh ways to communicate that purpose and to pursue it.

> We need to keep sufficiently informed to understand the context and nuances of events so we can initiate responses to unexpected threats and opportunities with confidence and judgment.

> It is our responsibility to understand what risks are acceptable for the organization and what risks are unacceptable.

> It is a failure of responsibility not to act when the risks are acceptable and the purpose and values of the group would have us act.

> It is a failure of responsibility to act when the risks are unacceptable and acting endangers the organization's purpose or violates its values.

Leaders usually support acts of initiative unless followers appear to be redirecting the spotlight to themselves at the leader's expense. If the initiative is motivated by service to the common purpose and not self-aggrandizement, leaders are prone to treat it with collegial respect—the follower is sharing the responsibilities of leadership.

INFLUENCING THE CULTURE

Every group has a distinctive culture: a set of norms for behaving and a way of looking at the world. Successful leaders and followers must learn the norms and respect the power of an existing culture. The stories of political appointees disregarding the culture of a bureaucracy and then being defeated by it are legion. But our universe and our cultures are interactive; a follower is not walking a one-way street. A courageous follower who respects a culture can also influence it.

Too often, a follower's instinct is to blend in and adapt to the attitudes of a group even if they are passive, cynical, or defeatist. Courageous followers don't allow their own values to be subsumed by the prevailing culture. We can influence the existing culture if we respect these principles:

> **Our willingness to stand out, to demonstrate differing attitudes, not as a challenge to the group but simply as an expression of our own outlook and vision, adds strength to the organization.**

> **Our appreciation and support of the values and traditions that give group pride and cohesion allow us to credibly model other characteristics not currently embraced by the group.**

> **By staying true to our own values and vision and linking these to the common purpose, we can influence the energy the group generates for accomplishing the purpose.**

> **Adhering to our own "higher" inclinations in a culture that doesn't obviously support them requires clarity of values and self-acceptance.**

A follower's ability to remain his own person while bonding with the group is the same ability that allows a follower to challenge the group or its leaders when the need to do so arises. Followers who successfully influence a group by modeling other behaviors in a nonconfrontational mode establish their integrity and earn the group's respect. They are in a strong position to challenge the group if that is needed at a future point.

BREAKING THE RULES

Effective followers assume responsibility for learning the rules of the system in which they operate. Rules are created as guidelines for using the group's resources, as methods for orderly decision making, as assurances of fairness, as clarification and guarantees of expected standards. Rules are the agreements by which the group maintains its identity, expresses its values, and coordinates its activities. An effective follower understands the rules and knows how to get things done within their framework.

Courageous followers also recognize the subordinate relationship of rules to purpose. They are alert to the evolution or interpretation of rules that may impede the accomplishment of the organization's purpose. They have an adult understanding of rules: they support rules when they serve the common purpose and question rules when they thwart the purpose.

Often, if we trace down the source of a rule that seems to violate common sense and obstruct service, we find it is being applied in a way that was never intended. Rules usually evolve in a historical context and, as the context changes, rules need to be reviewed for relevancy. Nothing more quickly tests our patience as customers than an employee telling us we can't do something that common sense demands be done. We sometimes wonder what is happening to the hundreds of millions of dollars spent on customer service programs when we encounter an employee obstinately insisting on "company policy."

Our attitude toward rules is critical. It affects our relationship to the leader and our response to the leader when questionable orders are issued. The following guidelines may help when we are confronted with rules that seem to thwart the organization's purpose or clash with its values:

> **It is not ethical to break rules for simple convenience or for personal gain, but neither is it ethical to comply with or enforce rules if they impede the accomplishment of the organization's purpose, the organization's values, or basic human decency.**

A courageous follower assumes responsibility in dilemmas where rules impede service and is willing to bend, circumvent, or break the rules to get things done.

When a rule impedes an organization's ability to give appropriate service, courageous followers do not hide their circumvention but use it as an example of why the rule must be vigorously reviewed.

Followers who find themselves hiding their circumvention of rules should carefully examine their motivations and assumptions. This type of deception is inappropriate in all but the most repressive of climates.

Courageous followers trust themselves, and are trusted by the organization, to be interpreters of the organization's values when applying a rule to a specific circumstance. Occasionally, at senior levels of government or private industry, we see individuals using the discretion entrusted to them to justify criminal acts. This, of course, is not an act of courage but a betrayal of the trust placed in them by the organization's stakeholders.

BREAKING THE MIND-SET

Sometimes, it is not just rules that need to be broken but the organization's whole mind-set. The pursuit of the common purpose may be hampered by the group's assumptions about the world. These assumptions are lenses through which the group filters information. Sometimes, the lenses also filter out important possibilities.

It is a great challenge to help a group escape the limits of its current mind-set; we are asking the group to make a leap into territory it doesn't even realize exists. Courageous followers who wish to present a new paradigm must carefully prepare the group to receive it, or they will be met with blank stares and quick rejections. The group doesn't have a framework on which to register and evaluate the ideas. For example, an organization that hasn't begun grappling with its lack of cultural diversity has no inkling of the real issues, let alone how they themselves contribute to the problem.

We must be willing to take our concerns about the organization's current paradigm to the highest level of leadership and begin creating awareness there of the issues. We need to prepare our resources well for creating this awareness and an awareness of alternative paradigms. These resources might include the following:

Statistics—the numerical facts about a group's current practice

Case histories and anecdotes

Comparison with other groups' practices

Outside experts and studies

Impact statements from affected stakeholders

Historical analogies

Tours and inspections of widely different models

Future scenarios of the extension of current practices

Once awareness is created, a courageous follower can enlist the group's energy to begin exploring new possibilities.

IMPROVING PROCESSES

Processes are the chains of activity through which an organization fulfills its needs and the needs of the individuals and groups with which it interacts. Core processes are what permit the organization to achieve its purpose, and other processes support these.

One danger in a group is that each member vaguely thinks someone else should do something about flaws they observe in its processes. Frequently, group members see inefficiencies but don't act on ideas they have for remedying them. Failure to act lowers a follower's sense of responsibility for what is occurring. Each follower thinks, "If I were in charge, I would do it differently, but I'm not in charge, so it's not my problem." Meanwhile, the common purpose suffers.

Courageous followers do not quietly ignore or ineffectively complain about wrongs they see. They do not assume that others also see these things and will correct them. They look for and find the avenues open to them for effecting change.

When considering responsibilities for the organization's processes, bear in mind these thoughts:

> Remedying a specific service complaint helps retain the individual customer's loyalty, but remedying the process that caused it saves the loyalty of many.

> If there is a clear process owner who has official responsibility for that process, our minimum responsibility is to ensure that the owner is aware of the process flaws we have observed.

> If there is no clear process owner or process improvement team, we should alert the organization to the need for one.

> Courageous followers don't just tell the leader "something should be done about this," adding to the burden of leadership, but present ideas for improving the process that the leader can consider.

Improving a process, such as the fulfillment of member requests in an association, the involvement of community groups in policy making, or the shortening of response time to customer orders, often requires a champion to focus the organization on the need for it and to ensure that the necessary follow-through occurs. A courageous follower is willing to be this champion.

TESTING YOUR IDEAS

Sometimes an organization isn't ready to address a deficiency or try a better way of doing things. Other needs seem more pressing. This can be frustrating to a follower who feels strongly about an issue. Throwing up our hands and giving up is not assuming responsibility. Our challenge is to find a way to test our ideas by putting them into action and demonstrating their potential. With determination and creativity, new processes and approaches can usually be piloted without a prohibitive expenditure of resources. Designing a pilot that can be conducted out of an existing budget simplifies or eliminates the initial approval process.

In addition to designing a sound pilot with good measurements, we need to pay attention to how we will build consensus for the idea if the pilot is successful. Our chances for gaining acceptance of the idea improve if we secure the early involvement of people whose opinion decision makers value. They will help us take our idea from the successful pilot stage to implementation.

If we are successful, we must remember to give plenty of credit to those who supported the pilot and to the leader who tacitly let us conduct it. If the idea flops, we learn from it and move on to the next idea. When we put our ideas on the line by testing them, we risk failure. When followers initiate and take risks, there is a healthy blurring of the line between followership and leadership.

3

THE COURAGE
TO SERVE

I NEVER CEASE TO BE AMAZED at how many decisions a good chief of staff makes for a U.S. senator without consultation. Given the hundreds of small and large requests a senator receives daily, this is an essential function. It is also the epitome of judgment in serving a leader: knowing when you can speak for the leader and when you had better consult her. It takes courage to serve as a close aide to a senior leader. If you bother leaders with too many matters, you will squander their energy; if you fail to bring things that they need to know to their attention, you may blindside them, causing embarrassment or calamity.

In many organizational cultures, when things go wrong, someone has to pay, to be offered up as a sacrifice, and it may be you. In the British and other governments, it is customary for a minister to resign if there has been a scandal that could tar the prime minister. Like chess, the bishops and rooks are offered to save the king.

At the same time, you may never get all of the credit for the hard work you do. Some of it is done in the leader's name, and it is she who presents the ideas to the board or the press. Yet if the leader falls from favor, as a close aide you may go down with her.

Some people prefer a safe backwater in the organization, and you can hardly blame them. Those closest to a leader often live with a high level of stress. One senator, who retained a consulting group I directed, has very high standards and equally volatile emotions. A minivan driver, who had been hired for the day to take the senator and some of his staff to a string of speaking engagements, listened as the senator repeatedly upbraided his staff about various details. "I get it!" the driver said to one of the staff who stayed behind during one speech. "You put up with this because they pay you a million dollars a year!" It was the only way he could imagine anyone would voluntarily put up with that kind of stress.

There is an art to serving a dynamic leader. Done well, with superior skill, both our stress level and the leader's can be kept down and creative energy can be maximized. Brilliant support contributes as much to an organization's ability to fulfill its purpose as does brilliant leadership. Too often, I've seen leaders grow increasingly overworked, frustrated, and ill-tempered. They haven't known how to get the support they need. Whether the leader asks for it or not, followers need to give the leader the support she needs and help her if she doesn't know how to accept it.

Serving a leader is a complex task. It demands a high degree of organizational know-how. It requires helping the leader manage time and information. It calls for vigorously projecting the leader's values and message. It asks for great judgment, even wisdom. And it can necessitate being very cool under fire.

In the years that I have conducted courageous follower workshops, I have learned that, too often, group members feel powerless to influence leaders and are too quick to dismiss leaders with whom they have become disenchanted. Sometimes, the first step to improving these relationships lies not in challenging the leader's behavior or policies, but in showing care and concern for the leader. Find ways to meet the leader's expectations and reduce her stress levels. When trust and goodwill are strengthened in this way, opportunities will present themselves in due course for addressing sensitive issues.

CONSERVING A LEADER'S ENERGY

Leaders occupy positions of high visibility and are often buffeted by powerful forces. Internal and external pressures build and can test or distort a leader's values and judgment. An important function of followership is minimizing unnecessary pressure that may contribute to this distortion.

Courageous followers help leaders make choices about demands that push their personal and professional lives out of balance. Leaders are often driven personalities; they use their bountiful energy to inspire or cajole the organization to fulfill its purpose. But this bountiful energy isn't boundless, even if the leader thinks it is. It must be conserved and renewed. Questions we should ask and consider include these:

What kinds of activities refresh the leader?

Is there sufficient time scheduled for these activities and is it vigorously defended?

What activities take the greatest toll on the leader's creativity and temperament?

> How can energy-draining activities be minimized or prepared for in ways that reduce the toll they take?
>
> How can we organize to permit the leader to focus more on high-payback activities?
>
> What functions has the leader always done that should now be delegated?
>
> What activities are central to the leader's role and should not be delegated but be better supported?

If internal pressure is driving the leader to do "too much," we must confront her with the consequences. If the leader is micromanaging, we must challenge her to trust more. With a micromanager, we should avoid slipping into a pattern of not attending to the details of our work "because the leader will change it anyway." This reinforces a leader's belief that she has to "do everything" and contributes to the downward spiral of overload and fatigue.

The courageous follower is willing to both comfort and confront the leader, to assume additional responsibilities to relieve the leader, or to initiate dialogue to help the leader examine her own contribution to the overload.

ORGANIZING COMMUNICATION PROCESSES

Appropriate organization is necessary to achieve the common purpose and to support the leader. From the most complex society right down to the individual cell, all life must organize itself. Higher life organizes itself around a vision, values, and goals. Effective followers help leaders clarify the vision and goals and develop the organization that the group needs to pursue them.

The most important organizational structures and processes are those concerning communication. They tell us how all other organizational processes are functioning. A survey of almost any organization shows that few leaders organize communication processes that are fully satisfactory to the group. To serve a leader well, we must help the leader detect communication deficiencies and design the right combination of communication vehicles to satisfy the organization's needs. The design of communication processes should be sensitive to multiple needs, including the need for

the leader to communicate her vision directly to all levels of the organization and its stakeholders;

stakeholders to be able to communicate their views to the leader;

mechanisms to summarize communication to a leader and help her prepare responses so she is not overwhelmed by volume;

information to move swiftly up, down, across, in, and out of the organization so no parts of the group or its environment are left unconnected;

information to circulate among all members of natural work groups so that class distinctions aren't created or reinforced;

information to be freely circulated, but not overcirculated so that it jams an organization's functioning or compromises its competitiveness;

the right combination of media and technologies to facilitate communication in an array of situations;

communication that leads to creativity, distributed decision making, coordination, implementation, and evaluation.

Continuous review is required to achieve balance in a communication system so that all levels are touched in a timely way, in all directions, without overburdening the leader or the organization.

ACQUIRING ACCESS

Obtaining the right amount of access to a leader requires striking a delicate balance. Followers must have or negotiate a certain degree of access to support a leader and perform their roles. But followers often desire more access than a leader can realistically give or than they necessarily need. We must be alert to our own ego-based desire for unnecessary access and keep this in balance so it does not put undue strain on a leader's time and energy. However, we should not allow our exaggerated sense of a leader's importance and time constraints to keep us from requesting access when it is appropriate for accomplishing critical tasks or building and maintaining our relationship.

We can bear in mind these guidelines for improving our access:

> If we genuinely require more access, we must make whatever access we already enjoy valuable to the leader.

> We must know our own communication weaknesses, such as rambling or getting too technical, that diminish a leader's willingness to grant needed access, and work to keep these weaknesses in check.

> Focusing on high-value issues and being well prepared are a baseline for improved access but are not necessarily sufficient.

> Relaxed but productive and stimulating interchange may recharge a leader in ways that formal meetings don't, causing the leader to seek out more contact with us.

> Candor can create further receptivity in a leader because it is too often lacking in the atmosphere surrounding prominent leaders.

> We should be aware of how the leader best receives and processes information and stress that vehicle—oral, written, electronic, graphic, experiential—to maximize the value of the access we do have.

Courageous followers empower themselves so they don't require excessive access to make decisions. Empowerment requires internal confidence and external assumption or negotiation of authority to support the common purpose. A robust relationship with the leader is needed to fulfill the potential of the follower's role. Appropriate access is both a requirement and a sign of that relationship.

THE RESPONSIBILITIES OF GATEKEEPING

Followers who control the access of other followers to a leader have the responsibility to use this power fairly. The power of proximity to power is itself intoxicating and can inflate egos. Gatekeepers need to guard against becoming arrogant and indifferent to the needs of those seeking access to the leader. If supporting a leader requires blocking or limiting access to an overloaded leader, a gatekeeper can do so with empathy and find other ways to help the person seeking access. A gatekeeper can become less a border guard and more of a traveler's aid station—a traffic router, networker, and facilitator.

Gatekeepers should not allow their own prejudices to insulate the leader from competing views or disapproved-of sources. We must guard against litmus tests or subtle cultural biases, which limit the diversity of ideas reaching a leader. A gatekeeper must also avoid biasing a leader's receptivity to a communication by introducing it derogatorily: "Oh, here's another memo from so-and-so." Biased remarks by a gatekeeper are a form of pandering to a leader's perceived prejudices or imposing one's own.

A gatekeeper who distorts the screening process or abuses the leader's reflected power hurts the leader and the organization. A courageous follower confronts this issue head on with the gatekeeper and, as necessary, with the leader. A functional gatekeeper protects those within the walls but freely lets in the commerce of ideas that keeps the community vibrant. A dysfunctional gatekeeper just keeps slamming doors.

Prominent leaders often receive many requests to lend their prestige to causes and events—charities, boards, coalitions, political activities, symposiums, civic initiatives. If leaders overcommit, they become distracted from the common purpose. Effective followers do not necessarily leave this larger gatekeeping process to one individual. They establish a process to insulate an in-demand leader from excessive pressure and help her make balanced choices about which invitations to accept, delegate, or decline. A schedule reflects a leader's values and priorities, and the process for developing it should not be taken lightly.

Competing scheduling requests can be batched and evaluated against well-thought-out criteria by a small, functionally balanced group. Some possible criteria are as follows:

What opportunity does this invitation present for advancing the organization's purpose?

What message does accepting or declining send about the leader's values?

What is competing with this opportunity for the leader's time and what value does that have to the organization?

Can the request be meaningfully delegated?

A well-thought-out scheduling process helps the leader and organization stay focused on the common purpose and the strategy for achieving it.

BUFFERING A LEADER

Great leaders face great challenges. They often encounter relentless opposition while seeking a path that will achieve their organization's purpose. Read the biographies of Winston Churchill, Martin Luther King, Jr., or Gandhi and you will find years of patience-wearing struggle and setbacks. Many less famous leaders also labor for years or decades before they see their dreams materialize.

We must take great care not to compound the real external challenges by relaying bad information and unsubstantiated rumors to a leader. These create an exaggerated perception of external pressure or hostility to which an inflamed leader may overreact. A follower who is in the habit of running to a leader with unsubstantiated rumors and gossip is serving some personal psychological need rather than serving the leader.

When confronted with alarming "news" for the leader, we might ask ourselves:

What do we actually know versus what we have been told?

Does it make sense, or do we need to corroborate it further?

Do we have both the facts and the context in which they occurred?

If an event actually occurred, what's behind it?

Should we accept the events at face value or explore if they have been manipulated to serve another agenda into which we are being drawn?

Is the information we have sufficient, or do we need to gather further information so we can make recommendations?

Once information has been substantiated, we should never protect a leader from bad news as it is an important source of feedback. When reporting bad news, we should attempt to provide the leader with options that support the group's value system as this will be a time when values are tested:

"This is what has occurred, and here are three options we've developed."

"The most expedient course is _____, but it doesn't serve our values and purpose well in the long run, so we recommend _____ ."

A steady stream of bad news may demoralize the leader and sap the will required to carry on. To balance the picture, we need to also present examples of how the leader's efforts and commitment to the common purpose are successful. Even small successes can sustain an embattled leader and group in their struggle.

DEFENDING THE LEADER

It is easy for people inside or outside the organization to target a leader because the leader is visible and represents the organization and its authority. Sometimes there is a lot of behind-the-back complaining about a leader. Although the complaints may be legitimate, this form of addressing them is not. It creates an atmosphere of diminished mutual respect, increased alienation, and lackluster implementation of strategy. When we encounter it we need to defend our leaders.

It is important for a group to remember its leader's strengths, which sometimes are forgotten or taken for granted. Whatever flaws a leader may have, her strengths may be holding the organization together or contributing significantly to the organization's purpose. A courageous follower who encounters chronic complaining challenges the group to remember the leader's strengths. We can give constructive feedback only from a perspective of true regard for the individual.

If we are among the complainers, a hard examination of our own role may be in order. Complaining may be a way of projecting onto the leader our frustration at not being more successful in our efforts. We need to examine how we can assume more responsibility and be more effective.

Complaining should not be ignored or repressed. There is something to learn from it. The courageous follower urges complainers to package and deliver their communications in useful ways rather than filling the air-waves with discontent.

BUFFERING OTHERS FROM A LEADER

Often such deference is paid to authority that the slightest comment made by a leader is taken literally. Leaders can be mortified to find an off-the-cuff comment they made was construed to be "policy," a one-time solution to a unique situation was interpreted as a change in standard procedure, or an angry reaction was conveyed as their final position. If an instruction from a leader seems to fly in the face of good sense, a follower at any level should request clarification before implementing it. This seems to be such common sense as not to deserve mention, but the principle is often violated by followers who have not yet found their own locus of responsibility.

If we work as a close aide to a leader, we have a special role to play in relaying communication from the leader. We must sometimes function as a step-down transformer, taking a high-voltage emanation from the leader and modulating it so it can be received usefully at its intended receipt point several levels down an organization. The leader would do the same if she were talking to people she only sees occasionally. Just as we often address new acquaintances with more circumspection than we do intimate friends, the different levels of comfort and familiarity some people have with the leader demand judgment in how we relay a leader's thoughts, feelings, and instructions. When we find ourselves in this facilitative role, these guidelines may help:

> **A leader's message should not be diluted, but it is our responsibility to understand the context in which it was delivered and how this differs from the context in which it will be received.**

> Facilitation may require faithfully interpreting and relaying the essential communication while modifying the quality of the carrier wave so that it can be received as intended.

> It is our responsibility to help others understand what the leader is communicating, and to detect and clarify false impressions that may block acceptance or implementation.

Literally relaying or thoughtlessly implementing all of a leader's instructions is not true support but an effective way of undoing a leader.

ACTING IN THE LEADER'S NAME

When we are a close aide to a leader, our acts are often perceived as extensions of the leader's values and intentions. In organizations in which the leader is focused on strategic and external priorities, we may become the primary contact point for the rest of the organization and exert great influence on it. Intentionally or not, we can create an atmosphere that doesn't reflect the leader's values.

Acting in the leader's name is a delicate affair. Yet we must be willing to do it. We need a high degree of awareness of how our tone and actions support or detract from the leader's values. If we allow our own issues with power to reflect poorly on the leader, we may do serious damage to the organization and, eventually, to our career. For example, if we are more prone to a rigid command-and-control style of management than the leader, and staff wants the organization to be more participatory, we may generate strong resentment toward "management." When the leader becomes aware of how this is weakening the group's commitment to the common purpose, she may need to dramatically distance herself from us.

By staying closely attuned to the leader, we can reflect her values and approve or initiate actions that are consistent with those values and goals without burdening the leader with details. Clarifying in advance the categories of decisions we will make can prevent overstepping our authority. We might ask ourselves these questions when considering if we can speak for the leader in specific situations:

What has the leader's position been on similar issues in the past?

Has the leader recently expressed clear feelings on this issue?

Is the leader in the process of reviewing her position on this issue?

Am I comfortable with what I perceive to be the leader's position on this?

Is there anything that makes this a special case warranting consultation?

We must be careful not to interject our own agendas in the leader's name. When courageous followers feel strongly about an issue and the leader does not, they take a stand on that issue in their own name and do not infer the leader's support for it. They appreciate the power conferred on them and do not abuse it by blurring the boundaries between themselves and the leader.

DEFINING A LEADER PUBLICLY

In many activities, an organization's supporters and adversaries form their opinion of the organization from the perception they have of its leaders. If the leader has an image that commands attention and respect, the organization is in a stronger position to achieve its purpose.

An effective organization does not wait for those outside the organization to define its leader's image. Outsiders often do so in light of their own agendas or based on isolated experiences. It is better to publicly define our own leaders in terms of their real strengths, values, achievements, and goals. At lower levels of leadership this may be as simple as mentioning these when we speak to more senior leaders or to leaders of other groups. At higher levels this may warrant an orchestrated public relations effort. Successful public relations uses only images built on reality. It is the leader's responsibility to live by the values she projects. It is our responsibility to help her do this.

We must not expect perfection from our leaders because doing so contributes to the delusion of the infallible leader. We are right to expect, however, that leaders substantively live up to the image we are projecting with their agreement. By confronting leaders about departures from their publicly stated values, we help them remain the people they want to be.

We must keep in mind several principles when projecting a leader's image:

> **We should never cover up a leader's behavior that does not conform to her public image.**

> **We should use the discrepancy between publicly held values and personal behavior as feedback to help a leader reexamine her values and behavior.**

> **Simultaneously, we should act to prevent the leader's detractors from redefining her image based on behavior that was an exception to her values and virtues.**

Reducing the complexity of a human being to digestible images is dangerous and difficult, but courageous followers recognize that this occurs and participate in the process with a deep regard for truth.

FOCUSING THE CREATIVE LEADER

A creative leader is a fount of ideas. This quality is of great value to an organization. But if followers attempt to indiscriminately implement all of a prolific leader's ideas, focus will be lost, and the leader and organization may become exhausted.

If the leader's ideas completely fill the group's agenda, there will be no room for followers to contribute their own creativity. It is a critical function of courageous followership to evaluate the flow of ideas from a leader and to determine which have the greatest potential for forwarding the common purpose. Criteria should be established for evaluating ideas and opportunities. The criteria may include the following:

> **Does this idea forward our core mission?**

> **How large is the potential payoff for our stakeholders?**

Will it drain resources from higher payoff activities?

Does it make the best use of our strengths and talents?

Will it leave us in a stronger position to fulfill our purpose?

Does it have serious downsides or entail unacceptable risks?

A process is needed to select the ideas that are real gems. We should energetically implement these and demonstrate to the leader how implementing the numerous other ideas will detract from the gems. If the leader is usually respectful of the evaluation process but convinced a particular idea should be pursued despite the trade-offs, courageous followers support her unless the risks are overwhelming. Creative intuition cannot always be subordinated to analytical processes.

PRESENTING OPTIONS

Even the most creative leaders appreciate it when others present them with options for handling situations. The options followers generate often circumscribe the range of actions a leader contemplates. The quality of those options makes a huge difference to the success of an organization. Neither we nor our leaders should settle for good ideas on important issues until we have energetically searched for great ideas.

Before we can present options, we need to be sure we are solving the right problem. What seems like an isolated problem is often one manifestation of a complex set of interactions within a system. We need to search for the questions that will unearth the fundamental problem instead of searching for solutions to the apparent problem. We can learn different systems for doing this, such as the Ishikawa cause-and-effect "fishbone diagram," or Kepner/Tregoe's situation-and-problem-analysis processes, or Stephen Brookfield's critical-thinking approach.

The courageous follower at times sounds like a philosopher:

What do we think we know?

Why do we think we know this?

What assumptions underlie our belief?

Under what circumstances are these assumptions valid?

Do the current circumstances approximate these?

How are they different?

What successful examples are there of operating on those assumptions?

What unsuccessful examples are there?

What can we learn from these examples?

Is there an entirely different way to think about this?

Is there something we can learn from thinking in a new way?

Can we draw analogies from unrelated fields that will further unlock our thinking?

In the best of worlds, the leader and group are open to this type of process. If they are not, we can ask these questions of ourselves and inject our answers into whatever dialogue exists.

What seems like the cause of a problem is often just the effect of a deeper problem. We can use the "rule of five whys" to get at the root of a problem, successively asking why something is so until a fundamental reason is uncovered:

Why did that occur?

Why was this so?

Why would that be so?

Why would that have been the case?

Why didn't we detect that sooner?

The need to identify the right problem must be balanced by the need to avoid analysis paralysis. Leadership requires making difficult decisions with incomplete data. The time comes for the follower to cease asking questions and to present concrete options. Depending on the urgency of the situation, this may occur in minutes or in months. Integrity is then served by following the "rule of three options."

Develop at least three good options for any situation.

By presenting several workable options, we give leaders genuine choices, not just the choices we want them to make.

If one choice presents ethical problems, we are less tempted to ignore the problems if we have other options.

The pros and cons of each option can be weighed, the benefits and dangers evaluated, and the best option or synthesis of options selected. Courageous followers help their leaders go beyond popular wisdom and search for fundamental understanding of issues, from which visionary leadership can develop.

KNOWING WHEN YOU DON'T KNOW

Followers can experience enormous psychological pressure to look good around a leader and provide answers to questions off the cuff. Our culture values the expert who can spout off opinions more than the sage who contemplates.

Courageous followers regard the act of advising as a trust. They differentiate between what they know factually, what they intuit, and what they don't know at all. They don't overstate their case.

"I've researched this and can tell you unequivocally that _____ ."

"I've met with them and know they feel strongly about that, so I advise against doing it."

"All I can tell you is what my gut says."

"My feeling is to go with _____, but I'd want to run it through a full decision-making process."

"I don't have a clear sense about that—let me think about it and get back to you."

"That's not my area of experience. Have you consulted _____ , who has worked a lot with that?"

If we are close to a leader, we can serve as a sounding board, reflecting back what we hear without pretending to have an expertise we lack:

"You sound uncomfortable with that idea. Are you?"

"From what I know of you, you tend to be cautious. Are you being overly cautious in this situation?"

"My sense is that you can trust him. Is there anything making you feel otherwise?"

"From what I've heard you say, your confidence seems justified."

"There's something that doesn't ring true. Can you clarify the situation a bit more?"

In this way, we can help a leader think through difficult issues or prepare for critical events despite our lack of expertise on a particular subject. Courageous followers are confident enough of their value to the leader that they do not need to inflate that value with pretended expertise.

AVOIDING INSULARITY

There is a danger that the very success of the leader-follower relationship may weaken a leader. Leaders who become comfortable with their closest followers may begin to rely only on them for information, counsel, and feedback. Insularity occurs, and both leader and followers lose perspective and freshness of ideas; the team grows stale. If we always see the same kind of people, we always have the same kind of ideas.

Many newly elected presidents of the United States surround themselves with lifelong friends. The impulse is understandable. Taken too far, however, it is dangerous and works against a leader. We are prone to surround ourselves with people whose experiences, ideas, and temperaments are compatible with ours. They are mirrors, albeit mirrors set at different angles. Mirrors are important, but in different situations we need a variety of optical devices to perceive and understand events: microscopes, telescopes, periscopes, spectroscopes, infrared night-vision equipment. Relying on one type of instrument permits us to see what that instrument is good at seeing. To use power well, we must see and understand events from many perspectives, at many levels.

As close aides, consciously or not, we may encourage the tendency of leaders to narrow their sources of counsel because this increases our own power. Our egos nudge the common purpose off center stage. It takes courage to welcome others, who may dilute our power, into the inner circle. By bearing in mind the following observations and guidelines, we may avoid complicity in the tendency to insularity:

> All humans long for greater power over their destiny; by serving a powerful leader who comes to rely on us, we feel more in control of our destiny.

> In our desire for our leader to be powerful and for ourselves to remain close to this power, we can blind ourselves to a leader's flaws and lose our ability to effectively provide feedback.

> Though it goes against our instinct for accruing power to ourselves, we must encourage a leader to periodically seek other perspectives without the filter of close followers.

> If we insulate the leader and ourselves from other perspectives, there is a far greater chance we will misuse and lose the power we desire.

Other perspectives provide a reality check on the relationship of a leader and close followers. Once followers move past feeling threatened, they, too, learn from the new perspectives; they, too, gain access to new ways of seeing. Diversity is a primary source of the balance needed to use power wisely.

ENCOURAGING PEER RELATIONS

No matter how healthy the relationship between a leader and followers, it is not a substitute for a leader's relationships with peers. Even a relaxed leader-follower relationship always has some tendency toward a little distance, a distinction in roles. We need to be alert to a leader who lacks peer relationships and encourage their development. Men, in particular, are not known for tending to their relationships. Sometimes as they move up the ladder, they leave friends behind and wind up instead with associates.

Some leaders mix socially in their professional circles. While important, this tends to be a business or political activity. They are presenting their social personae. Leaders need relationships that get below the surface, relationships that allow them to talk about their vulnerabilities as well as their strengths.

The need for peer relations exists for all leaders, but it is critical for charismatic leaders such as religious figures whose followers' devotion blinds them to their flaws. We have seen the number of evangelical ministers who have fallen from grace in recent years. Courageous followers must encourage charismatic leaders to cultivate relationships with others who do not hold them in awe.

It may require someone who has known the leader in different roles and stages of development to "get through" to him. It may require someone of similar stature to empathize with and challenge him. He may just need a buddy to have a heart-to-heart talk with. A close relationship with just one peer can also present a problem, however, if the relationship mutually reinforces an unhealthy condition such as sexism or alcoholism. A diversity of peer relationships avoids undue influence by one individual. Peer relationships might include the following:

A longtime friend or relative

Other prominent leaders in the same or related fields

A former follower who has become a leader of comparable stature

A former mentor who reestablishes a relationship with the leader

A peer support group, such as a monthly roundtable in which business leaders discuss their problems

A spiritual counselor or issue expert who can speak to a leader on equal terms

It is not the role of followers to engineer a leader's social relations. But it is the role of courageous followers to stay alert to a leader's well-being. Isolation from peers is a warning sign that should be heeded.

MANAGING CRISES

We often hear that a leader's job in a crisis is to keep the environment calm enough so that people can get their work done. Followers also have this responsibility: to be productive and supportive while a path is charted through the crisis. Often, events unfold too rapidly for a leader and followers to fully consult with each other before acting. Trust and morale can be strengthened or shattered depending on responses made in these trying conditions.

Crisis preparation is a key tool in crisis management. For example, we can determine likely scenarios in which the leader or followers may need to make important decisions. Then we can develop and record guidelines for emergency responses that adhere to our values. In addition, in an acute crisis, we must be prepared to give the leader or acting leader complete support. In a rapidly unfolding situation, we may need to suspend our responsibility to fully understand what we are being asked to do before we act. This itself is an act of courage.

If normal decision support processes are suspended, it is important that the group reassert these at the earliest possible moment. We must be careful the curtailed consultation demanded by an emergency response doesn't become a new norm due to recurring crises. Recurring crises are a glaring sign of poor management, which must be analyzed and remedied.

There is a distinction between recurring crises and a prolonged crisis. A prolonged crisis, such as one stemming from a faulty product and the years of litigation and adverse publicity it generates, may reflect a specific management error that has long since been corrected. Nevertheless, the duration of the fallout from the error may erode the leader's and group's morale through constant buffeting. The instinct for individual self-preservation may threaten to pull apart the organization. If stress has attenuated the leader's capacity for facing the public and rallying the organization, we may have to compensate for the leader.

Our actions to support the leader and hold the organization together should include the following:

Reaffirming the group's sense of purpose as a context in which to absorb the crisis

Unburdening the leader of usual or extra duties if the emotional stress of the crisis is threatening the leader's ability to function

Keeping the group fully and honestly briefed on actual and anticipated developments to reduce rumors and shocks

Isolating the contact points in the organization to those designated and trained to specifically deal with the crisis, so the rest can get their work done

Using the crisis to spur self-examination by the organization so that reforms to address underlying causes can be initiated

Helping the group, after the acute phase of the crisis has passed, to process any trauma.

If we assumed leadership prerogatives during a crisis, we should be attentive to relinquishing them when the crisis is over unless our formal authority has been expanded. Failure to do so can generate confusion and mistrust. An organization that manages a crisis well strengthens the bonds between leaders and followers. An organization that doesn't may simply form painful scar tissue.

WHEN THE LEADER IS ILL

The stress of leadership is high. It takes a physical as well as psychological toll. Drug or alcohol addiction is particularly problematic, but digestive problems, hypertension, sleep disorders, or migraine headaches can also interfere with a leader's performance or be aggravated by pressures on the leader. Different types of illness have different durations and complications. Each poses its own challenge to followers, from a six-week bout with Lyme disease to a survived heart attack, a battle with cancer, or progressive dementia.

Though serious illness can strike at any age, it is more common as people grow older. Senior leadership positions tend to be filled with older, more experienced people. Thus, illness among leaders is more common than we think. A close follower is faced with a special type of crisis when the leader is ill. The support a leader needs can become more demanding and pose new problems.

In lower levels of leadership, the challenge is often how to keep things going in the leader's absence or unburden her sufficiently so she can get the rest needed to recover. As in a crisis, we must decide what responsibility and authority is appropriate for us to assume.

In higher levels of leadership, the problem can become complicated because the attending physician may also be a follower who is balancing medical and business or political priorities. A head of state always has a personal physician. Often, so do other senior-ranking officials, celebrities, or wealthy industrialists. Sometimes great pressure is exerted on the physicians and the inner circle to collude in masking a medical condition from the public. It can be extremely dangerous to allow leaders to make high-level decisions, perform critical negotiations, or engage in taxing events when their physical and mental processes are impaired by illness, pain, or medication. Just as other courageous followers need our support from time to time, so may the leader's physician. When supporting a leader who is ill, we can bear in mind these guidelines:

> **Our primary responsibility is to the common purpose and those whom the organization serves.**

> **We are also responsible for the welfare of the leader as a human being who is ill, and perhaps in pain and frightened.**

> **When a leader won't acknowledge the seriousness of her illness, we must help her do so or turn to whatever institutional recourse is available.**

> **If the leader will be unavailable for a period, we must clarify responsibilities and authorities so the organization can function.**

> **The leader needs reassurance that her interests and the interests of the organization are being taken care of so that she can concentrate on recovery.**

If we fail to temporarily reorganize in the face of a leader's illness, the organization can badly drift. If we regroup for the duration of the illness, we can make forward motion toward our purpose. When it's clear that the leader's team is in control of events, those who might otherwise take advantage of the leader's impairment will be dissuaded from doing so.

Illness tests leaders and followers. It is part of life. It must be acknowledged and dealt with both medically and organizationally. Faced with a leader's illness, the courageous follower takes energetic action to care for both the leader and the organization.

CONFLICT BETWEEN LEADERS

An African proverb states, "When elephants fight, it is the grass that suffers." When pursuing an organization's purpose, conflict will naturally occur. If managed well, it can be productive. Conflict can also occur around ego issues, thinly masked in the guise of purpose. This is destructive conflict. When conflict occurs between two strong leaders who each have a large investment in the outcome of an issue—civic leaders, union presidents, heads of government—many people are at risk of getting trampled.

Turf war can take a great toll on a leader. Whereas some people appear to thrive on it, turf war absorbs creative energies and often leaves reputations and organizations wounded. The best chance of avoiding this destructive conflict, or ending it early, resides with the leaders' closest followers.

Warring leaders will apply emotional pressure for followers to support their positions. Loyalty may seem to demand that followers give in to the pressure, but the common purpose suffers if we do. Our higher responsibility is to help our leader find a course that serves the organization well. In doing so, our leader benefits, too. We can ask questions to put the issue into perspective:

> What are the interests of each leader in this situation? What are the interests of the stakeholders?

> Is continued conflict the best way of serving these interests, or are there alternatives?

What are the risks in escalating the conflict?

What is the common ground between the leaders that can be built on?

Is there anything our side is doing to exacerbate the conflict?

What is the key thing each leader needs from the other to let go of the matter?

There are times, however, when asking these questions just of our own leader is insufficient. The acts of the rival leader (public accusations, false statements, deceitful maneuvers) may continue to throw our leader into extreme positions. It is a mistake in this situation to assume that the entire camp of the rival leader is supporting these inflammatory actions. In fact, we might assume that at least some of the rival's followers are trying to bring their leader back into balance.

Therefore, the power to deescalate the conflict may well lie with us. It takes courage to suggest talking with "the enemy" when tempers are flaring. But the best approach may be to open a dialogue with the rival leader's followers about deescalating the conflict. Working together, courageous followers from opposing camps may defuse their leaders' destructive conflict and avoid the damage caused by territorial feuds. In this way, each organization's purpose and leaders are well served.

FORMAL CHECKUPS

If leaders stumble, courageous followers help to pick them up and repair them. But we support a leader better when we practice preventive medicine.

It is wise to get a physical checkup periodically even though we feel healthy. We look in the mirror daily and know generally that we are well, but a formal medical checkup looks deeper, searching for incipient problems. It uses instruments to measure what our senses can't readily detect. It is also wise for leaders to get checkups on how they are serving their organizations.

It takes courage for leaders to engage in a checkup process, as they don't know what it will uncover. Is there serious hidden disease? But just as the fear of cancer or heart disease warrants the periodic medical checkup, so should concern about the tendency of power to distort behavior motivate the leadership checkup. When problems with power or relationships are caught early, they are highly treatable; left to fester, they may prove fatal.

Various instruments for examination are available in the human resource department or through consulting firms. They measure a leader's own and others' perceptions of the leader's behavior and impact. Followers should encourage leaders to use these instruments. Feedback distilled from a wide range of perspectives can serve as the equivalent of sophisticated bioimaging tests, examining many cross sections of leadership dynamics.

If the leader isn't accustomed to these types of checkups, the courageous follower makes a strong case for them. If the information gleaned is used sensitively and skillfully, it can save the leader and organization future grief, as does most preventive medicine.

There are many ways to support a leader. Courageous followers use the range of tools at their disposal. Our motivation in each case is our commitment to the common purpose and our regard for the leader.

BUILDING RELATIONSHIPS WITH LEADERS

In the final analysis, a follower's potential for influencing a leader will depend on the quality of relationship that has been developed between them. There is a certain paradox in building such relationships. On the one hand, taking care to build a relationship with the leader is a strategic move. On the other hand, relationships are not the result of strategic maneuvering; they are born and grow through genuine concern for others and through cumulative experience that develops mutual appreciation and trust.

Relationships cannot be forced or willed into being. But they can be tended to and thoughtfully developed. Relationships cannot be manufactured by morphing ourselves into what we think the other wants us to be. The ploy is always transparent and backfires. We become someone whom the leader instinctively cannot fully trust. We must be ourselves, even if that requires discovering who we are and what we stand for.

Sometimes, followers who have a lot to offer fail to form a relationship with a leader that permits them to contribute all that they can. This may be traced to biases on the leader's part over which the follower has little control. But, just as often, the reason lies in some aspect of the follower's own character and way of relating to the leader. The follower is too anxious to please, too long-winded in explanations, too mired in details, too combative with politically important colleagues, too defensive—the possibilities are endless. Soliciting feedback and being open to self-reflection as discussed earlier can help. But it is still difficult to see ourselves as others do and what it is about our style that works against developing the foundations of trust and confidence with a leader.

Another approach to this challenge is to pay careful attention to others who appear to have successfully won a leader's trust. This may appear contradictory to the advice to be more our "true" self. But sometimes we need comparisons with others to learn about ourselves. When we travel to another culture, for example, we find ourselves becoming conscious of aspects of our own culture that we only begin to see in contrast to the other.

Here are some things we can pay attention to about ourselves and others that may help us, over time, to become one of a leader's trusted partners:

Who seems to serve both the leader and the common purpose in ways that the leader readily accepts?

What do they do that contributes to the leader being so receptive to their input?

How does this contrast with our own approach?

Is there something we can learn that will allow us to improve the quality of our own approach to the leader?

Is there a way to adapt what we observe to the reality of who we are?

What will it take for us to integrate this change so it is natural and sustainable?

If our own efforts to support a leader are generally or occasionally well received, what contributes to our success, and how can we reinforce this?

Service to a leader requires the intention to give service. But intention alone is insufficient. As Baldesar Castiglione counseled some five hundred years ago, it is only through a relationship of service to the leader, rendered in ways the leader can appreciate and value, that a follower builds the platform from which to meaningfully influence the tone and performance of the leader's tenure.

Castiglione knew that service is an art. Art is developed through commitment and discipline. If you choose to be a courageous follower, don't be careless about how you serve a leader. Take pride in this aspect of your role, and perform it with as much care and consistency as possible. People who serve others well in any capacity are highly attentive to the needs of those they serve, whether large or small. Good leaders know they are there to serve their followers, and courageous followers take equally good care of their leaders. Both work artfully and authentically in the service of the common purpose.

4

THE COURAGE
TO CHALLENGE

FOLLOWERS WHO PROVIDE robust support for leaders are in a strong position to challenge their actions that threaten the common purpose. Of the two broad areas in which we must be willing to challenge a leader—behavior and policies—the most difficult is behavior. It truly requires courage.

When I joined a struggling nonprofit organization, its entrepreneurial executive director had a plan to convert it into the marketing arm of a for-profit start-up. He had raised several hundred thousand dollars of venture capital, and it seemed to him a good solution to the needs of both organizations. When he described the plan to me, I thought it was ill advised. The start-up would need a year or two to develop the software for its niche market, and there was no guarantee it would succeed. Although the nonprofit was struggling, it had a history of being able to raise funds; it would no longer be able to do that if it gave up its tax-exempt status. This could kill the organization, which had a worthy purpose.

I was new to the organization, but I was comfortable giving my feedback to the executive director, as there was nothing personal about it. The executive director accepted my feedback and put the plan on hold. It was a good thing, too, because the start-up folded in a couple of years and the nonprofit has resurged and is going strong decades later.

In contrast, when I worked in a large organization, I encountered an influential and abusive division leader whom I didn't know how to stand up to, despite my years of service. She constantly disparaged members of other divisions, which divided and distracted the other divisions from the common purpose. She held a lot of political power in the organization and was personally very intimidating. Although I came from another division, I had her ear and might plausibly have given her the feedback she badly needed. But I couldn't bring myself to give her such sensitive, critical feedback about her personal behavior.

The story has two unhappy outcomes. One is that eventually I lost her ear and became one more victim of her venom toward "the other divisions." The other is that she continued to damage morale and, after involving the organization in illegal activity, was criminally indicted, dismissed from the organization, and served a prison term. If I had possessed the courage to challenge her, could I have changed this course of events? Only possibly, but I think that "possibly" makes trying worthwhile.

Devoted leaders and followers enter a type of sacred contract to pursue their common purpose. They both are guardians of that purpose. Part of the courageous follower's role is to help the leader honor this contract.

If we do not challenge a leader about dysfunctional behavior, the contract is slowly shredded before our eyes. The longer we wait, the less is left of the contract.

When we do not stand up to leaders, not only does the purpose suffer, so does our esteem for the leaders. This makes it harder to effectively give them feedback because it is difficult to do so when a relationship has deteriorated. The world may see a leader's attractive public persona, but, as in marriage, those closest to the leader also see the less attractive patterns. If we do not air our concerns about behavior that threatens the common purpose, we begin to define leaders by these unattractive characteristics rather than by their talent and commitment. It is the responsibility of partners in a relationship not to let this happen.

In my corporate consulting, I find it painfully common for staff not to tell their bosses what they need from them to do a good job: mundane things like holding fewer meetings and making them shorter, or giving fewer orders and letting people concentrate on getting the most important tasks done. Corporate leaders would be absolutely amazed at what they don't hear, because they'd find most of it inoffensive and worth considering. As followers, we need to start challenging our leaders on this level of process and policy when warranted. That will improve the organization's operation, strengthen the honesty of our relationship with the leader, and prepare us to deal with more difficult personal issues, should they arise.

Leaders with the strong egos and passionate vision needed to scale mountains are prone to self-deception. Some dynamic leaders are so invested in making their mark that they cannot let in information telling them it cannot be made in this way, at this time. A key role of a follower is to minimize this self-deception, to find ways of revealing reality to the leader. To stand up and remove the blinders from a leader's eyes is a daunting task when the leader is convinced he possesses X-ray vision.

In this chapter I present methods for getting through to leaders so they can hear what we have to say. I will discuss how to create the conditions for providing both effective feedback and timely input that is given the consideration it warrants. The extreme importance of the courageous follower overcoming groupthink impulses is explored, as well as several serious dysfunctional behaviors that followers may encounter and need to deal with.

If we find the courage to stand up to our leaders, they may initially find it as uncomfortable as we do, but eventually they will see that we are also standing alongside them in their corner.

EFFECTIVE LEADERSHIP BEHAVIOR

Leaders occupy their positions because of some constellation of strengths. Many of these strengths are of great value to the organization. Other strengths may not be those the organization needs at this time, at least not in the intensity the leader is using them. For example, the organization may have benefited from great force of personality during its founding days and now requires more collaborative skills in its leaders. But if a leader believes certain behaviors were responsible for earlier successes, he will tend to rely on those behaviors in his current role.

Like all of us, leaders believe their actions are justified, or they wouldn't take them. In the leader's case, the evidence seems irrefutable—their leadership behavior got them where they are now! This conviction forms a barrier to self-examination. They don't notice that the current context differs from earlier contexts in which the approach was successful. Taking action that may have been appropriate at other places or times may be inappropriate now. A governor's hands-on management style may serve a small state well, but a governor elected president of the country needs to learn the limits of that style.

An incident in which old successful leadership behavior clashes with a changed environment can provide a courageous follower the opportunity to discuss these changes with a leader. The fallout from the incident may provide a ripe opportunity for helping the leader reexamine behavior. If events have piqued a leader's interest in the subject, a close aide might formally or informally guide the leader through this thought process:

> **In what situations has the leader been most successful?**
>
> **What did the leader do in those situations that brought success?**
>
> **What are the similarities between those situations and the current one?**
>
> **What are the differences?**
>
> **How important are the differences?**
>
> **Has the leader been using any of the same strategies used in the earlier situations?**
>
> **Are those strategies working as well as they previously did?**
>
> **Given the different situations, what changes might improve the results?**

This nonthreatening approach invites leaders to examine what is working and what isn't, what is appropriate and effective in the current environment and what isn't. We are not offering feedback, simply asking questions that help leaders analyze the results they are getting with their current leadership methods. Skillful questioning is the mildest form of challenge to inappropriate behavior, but it is potentially extremely effective.

PREPARING A LEADER FOR FEEDBACK

Feedback is the great mechanism of self-discovery. We take an action, watch its effects, and learn what works and what doesn't. When we are young, this mechanism operates brilliantly.

As we develop and form our self-image, we start screening out feedback that contradicts that image. Preserving our internal sense of self becomes more important than learning and growth. We also may develop an external image we work to maintain. For those who become public figures—CEOs, principals, commanding officers, managing partners, politicians—protecting this public image may seem most important. More screens go up, and the only messages that penetrate are the ones that validate our image of ourselves.

There is little value in standing up and giving leaders feedback they cannot hear. The courageous follower's role is to find ways leaders can receive the feedback they need. We can minimize defensiveness by prefacing our feedback with a defusing statement that conveys respect and reminds the leader of the value of honesty:

> "You know how highly I think of your work, and I hope you won't mind my speaking frankly."

> "You know that I respect what you are trying to do, and I'm sure you'd want me to be honest with you."

Leaders are more apt to pay attention to feedback if we link it to outcomes they desire, to what motivates them. Is it promotion? Profits? Reelection? Reputation? We certainly hope the list includes the common purpose. By linking our feedback about a behavior or policy to its impact on what leaders value, their interest in the subject outweighs the impulse to defend their image:

> "I think what you are doing will affect _____ [what the leader values]. May I give you my views?"

> "I'd like to give you feedback on that. I think it's important to what you're trying to accomplish."

> Another way to defuse defensiveness is to share our own struggles with the same or similar issues. We can point out similarities between our situations as well as differences. This creates empathy and may help the leader talk about the subject.

> "I understand what you're up against as I had a similar experience with _____ ."

"I identify with your reaction because I have the same reaction when _____ ."

Giving a leader feedback about policies is usually easier than giving feedback about behavior, but not always. A leader may be completely wedded to a position that could have disastrous consequences. If a leader seems closed to hearing other viewpoints on an issue, we might approach the leader this way:

First say, "I have several things to tell you that you may not want to hear, but this is why you need to hear them."

Then state the reasons why the leader should listen, including the potential consequences to his own interests and to the common purpose.

Only give feedback on policies when you have the leader's attention and he has a somewhat open mind.

Preparing a leader for feedback is the requisite to effectively giving that feedback.

GIVING A LEADER FEEDBACK

We need to give leaders feedback with the same care we prepare them for it. Poorly given feedback can be received as an attack rather than a caring act. The leader may strike back defensively, dissuading the follower from giving future feedback.

Negative feedback must be clearly directed at the specific behavior or policy, not at the leader himself. It is better for a follower to say, "When you never smile at people, it makes them anxious" than to say, "You intimidate people." The leader can't change who he is, but he can change his behavior, smile occasionally, and help the people around him relax.

When giving feedback about behavior, we must clearly state:

what the specific behavior is;

what adverse effects it is causing;

how serious the potential consequences are should the behavior continue.

To reduce defensiveness, it is more effective to make statements relating how the person giving the feedback feels ("I" statements) than statements about what the person receiving the feedback is doing ("You" statements):

> **"My research shows that this policy will have several adverse consequences" rather than "Your policy will have adverse consequences."**

> **"I feel strongly about honesty and think we should reveal the information we have immediately" rather than "You're being dishonest by withholding the information."**

The "I" statements are truer and more effective. They don't sound accusatory so are less likely to trigger defensiveness.

Of course, it's preferable to raise sensitive issues privately with leaders just as we prefer them to do with us. Doing so is difficult if a prominent leader is always surrounded with aides. We may need to request a private audience or make a judgment call about giving feedback with others present.

It is important not to overdo feedback as we risk making the leader too introspective. Leadership requires looking outward and forward. Some people counsel making five positive statements for every criticism if we want healthy relationships. Whether this exact number is necessary, the principle seems sound. If someone gives us constant negative feedback, the practice wears thin and we close ourselves off.

It is not appropriate or realistic to expect leaders to accept every piece of feedback and immediately make changes. Feedback is not always on target. Sometimes the feedback is on target, but the timing is wrong. Sometimes leaders need to stick to their positions. Leaders who change their position every time they talk to someone else aren't leading.

Feedback is a critical and fragile element in the leader-follower system. Leaders are fortunate to have followers who develop this skill and understand its appropriate use.

GIVING A LEADER INPUT

Feedback is given in response to actions taken. Input advises on actions being contemplated.

Leaders do not need to solicit widespread input on every decision they make. But it is respectful and useful to solicit input from those who have responsibilities in the area that the decision will impact. If followers are to be responsible for certain spheres of activity, they have the right to be consulted on decisions related to that activity. In some cases, it may be helpful or necessary to ask for explicit agreements on this point when accepting a position.

In other cases, followers may find themselves in situations where they were not appropriately consulted and then need to negotiate this point with the leader. In such a case, it is usually more important to negotiate the principle for future action, rather than to attempt reversing a decision already taken. Ideally, the principle established will not simply be a bilateral agreement between the leader and follower, but a commitment to include all key players who will be impacted by a decision. The rules for giving effective feedback clearly apply to this conversation.

Assuming that a follower has skillfully made the case for prior consultation and the leader has agreed, followers can reinforce this commitment:

> "That's an extremely interesting idea. Thank you for giving me the opportunity to raise some concerns I have."

> "That's an interesting idea that will affect several divisions. I suggest that we explore it at the staff meeting."

> "You're raising an important point. Let me solicit some other perspectives to make sure we're not looking at this too narrowly, and then get back to you."

> "That sounds promising, but I'm disappointed you acted unilaterally when we've agreed that strategy changes will be reviewed at the senior management meeting."

> "We've got a problem. If you keep acting outside the process we've established, I and the other members of the team can't give you the creative ideas you want."

It is up to followers to be clear about the value they place on consultation and participation. Leaders are politically shrewd. When their people feel strongly about something, they usually won't ignore it.

CHALLENGING INDIRECTLY

We can't always create an environment in which upward feedback or input is readily accepted. Sometimes a leader feels threatened by direct confrontation or doesn't value participatory processes. We may need to find ways that engage rather than alarm the leader when we want to challenge questionable ideas or behaviors. The problem is often the leader's fixation on one idea, solution, or viewpoint. These are the blinders that have undone leaders throughout history.

A courageous follower chooses the right tool to help a leader examine options and their potential consequences. It is important to expand our toolkit so that we have the ability to indirectly challenge ideas and behaviors if that elicits dialogue rather than defensiveness. Anything that gets the leader to step a little to the side in viewing something is helpful. It begins a questioning process that can reveal flaws in the plan, unearth ways of proofing it against failure, enhance its potential, or lead to better alternatives. Simple questions we may ask to shift perspective include these:

"Is there another plausible interpretation of what has occurred?"

"Is there another way we can look at this situation?"

"Does anyone have a different take on this?"

Another indirect approach is to pose questions that others might ask the leader about his policy or behavior. Rather than directly challenging the leader, we are preparing him for challenges others may make in the less supportive arena outside the inner circle. A follower should become adept at asking "questions we might expect":

"How would we respond to the concern that _____?"

"Could that appear to conflict with our values on _____?"

"How might _____ interpret that?"

"How would we answer charges that _____?"

"What alternatives might our stakeholders want us to consider?"

"What would we say if asked about other options we considered and why they were discarded?"

Once a dialogue is opened, the leader's and followers' underlying concerns can surface, options can be explored, pros and cons weighed, possible outcomes tested. Even leaders who are open to creative challenge will find "questions we might expect" helpful in clarifying their positions.

AVOIDING KNEE-JERK REJECTION

Some people automatically reject new ideas or feedback. It doesn't matter what the idea is, it gets rebuffed. This is a version of the "not invented here" syndrome.

People who have been around awhile may be quick to say, "We've already tried that, and it didn't work." It's not a considered rejection of the idea so much as a reflex. Even if they have already tried something, maybe times have changed or there's a different way to do it that will be successful. Being too quick to say "It won't work" shuts them off from exploring the idea and supporting continuous improvement.

A leader's "knee-jerk rejection" of ideas may just be a poor habit a follower can work around until the leader unlearns the habit. Like any habit, it takes time to shake. If we know a leader is prone to knee-jerk rejection we can try a "delayed response" tactic:

Briefly air our observations and recommendations with the leader.

Quickly, without engaging in extended dialogue, ask the leader "to think about it" so that the issue can be further discussed at a later point.

Even if the leader's automatic rejection mechanism triggers, ask the leader to "still think about it."

Don't ask for and don't accept an immediate response or decision.

We shouldn't be surprised if the leader raises the issue with us again and displays openness to our ideas once he has given them some thought. By getting out of his face, we let an internal dialogue occur that seems to shift the "win-lose" framework from which he originally viewed our suggestion or request. Reflection replaces reflex. And we can raise the issue again if the leader doesn't, often with success.

Followers who find themselves too quick to reject ideas or feedback can use the same tool. Instead of disagreeing, we can say, "Let me think about that." If we really do think about it, we often find something in the idea we can use.

OVERCOMING GROUPTHINK

It is not only leaders who need to be challenged; sometimes a courageous follower must challenge the thinking of the whole group. Some groups are fractious and need help focusing on the common purpose. Other groups are cohesive; the members closely support each other, giving the group strength. Cohesiveness can become a weakness, however, if this close support develops into the need, almost regardless of cost, for unanimity. The value placed on concurrence supplants the central purpose of the group and becomes its primary, though unstated, agenda. Ideas that conflict with the group's policies and actions are, at best, offered weakly and withdrawn quickly if opposed. This phenomenon is known as *groupthink*.

A symptom of groupthink is a group self-image of infallibility and superiority: "Whatever we do is excellent. What other groups do is inferior." Groupthink screens out data and views that challenge this image. It eases out people who express divergent perceptions. The group becomes obsessed with its cleverness and importance, its power and image. It develops the illusion it is invulnerable to danger. Political and economic history is strewn with examples of the consequences of groupthink. The more subtle tyranny of groupthink replaces the more obvious tyranny of authoritarian leadership.

Courageous followers should periodically encourage a group and its leader to question themselves:

Have we objectively compared ourselves with similar groups lately, or do we just believe we are superior?

Are we using the right measures of success?

Are our measures consistent with our purported values?

Are we relying solely on self-measurement, or are we asking those we serve to evaluate us?

Are pressures to demonstrate performance leading to inflated performance statistics?

Have we grown complacent about searching for new ways of accomplishing our purpose?

Are other organizations doing innovative things that we should also consider?

Have we become so sure of ourselves that we no longer critically evaluate even risky ideas or pay attention to warning signals?

Are newcomers having to conform to our ways or are we also learning from them?

Are we failing to treat changes in our environment seriously because we don't think they can affect us?

Groupthink causes self-censorship. We do not permit ourselves to acknowledge our own divergent thoughts. We relinquish responsibility for our unique perspectives, which is a terrible error. If other members of the group accept the organizational status quo, we invalidate our own discomfort with it, even if the status quo dramatically departs from our ideals.

To rise above groupthink, we must trust ourselves. Trusting ourselves doesn't mean trusting that we are right but trusting that we are relevant, that our perceptions are keen, that we have verified our facts, that our thoughts are meaningful and important. It is only the individual who can rise above groupthink and help the cohesive group and its leaders test their ideas and actions against reality. We need to pay attention to our "inner voice":

Am I uncomfortable with things others seem to accept?

Am I accepting things I would not accept in another environment?

Am I devaluing information that contradicts what is supposed to be happening?

Am I inhibited from acting on my perceptions because no one else seems to share them?

If we aren't confident enough to voice our feelings strongly, we can raise them tentatively and observe the responses we get. Do the responses satisfy or reinforce our concerns? If the group and leader dismiss our points out of hand, we should continue to be concerned. If they genuinely address the points we raise, we are probably not dealing with groupthink.

THE DUTY TO OBEY

If we have courageously but unsuccessfully challenged a leader's policies, where do we stand in relation to implementing them?

The policies may be different from those we would have chosen; they may be fraught with risks with which we are uncomfortable; we may feel they have a negligible chance of success. These are our views—they may or may not be right. The leader may be displaying brilliant prescience, which we do not share. Only time will reveal the outcome. What is our responsibility in this situation?

If we choose to continue being a follower of this leader and if the policies are not morally repugnant to us, we have the responsibility to implement the policies. It takes courage to follow leaders when we are not convinced they are right, courage to truly allow leaders to lead. It is our responsibility to give the policy a chance, to make it work through energetic and intelligent adaptation rather than allow it to fail through literal interpretation or lukewarm execution.

We have the right to challenge policies in the policy-making process; we do not have the right to sabotage them in the implementation phase. In the world of politics, we often hear of leaks to the media intended to thwart a policy set by superiors or to forward the preferred policies of a subgroup. Those who intentionally undermine their leader's efforts are no longer followers; they are opponents.

Each of us has the right to become an opponent. But if we do so covertly, without declaring our opposition, while still holding our position and demeanor as a follower, we create havoc within the organization. We drive trust below a level where the group can remain cohesive. We create the opposite of a groupthink situation. We create factions and internal warfare that can threaten to immobilize or fracture the group and undermine the common purpose.

If we follow too slavishly, we contribute to blind groupthink. If we can't follow at all, we contribute to anarchy. If an organization is rife with leaks and acts of internal sabotage of the leader's policies, a courageous follower needs to look for the underlying reasons:

> **Is the policy-making process unfriendly to honest, diverse input, encouraging disaffected players to circumvent the process?**

> **Is there lack of sufficient respect in the organizational culture for the policy-making process, and an inclination to nullify its outputs?**

> **Are one or more players unwilling to follow and support team decisions?**

If the process for input into decision making is so weak it breeds discontent, we may need to further challenge the leader to open it up. If it is already credible and open, we may need to help the leader challenge individuals who are disregarding it or challenge the organizational culture itself to value it more.

Where serious disagreement exists, courageous followers may need to become courageous opponents. In all but the most repressive regimes, however, followers cannot become saboteurs and be called courageous.

CHALLENGING ABUSE EARLY

In addition to challenging policies, we may have to challenge behavior that violates our values and undermines the common purpose. Corruption of values doesn't occur all at once. Usually, a series of small departures from an individual's values leads to larger departures. The nonprofit director's use of an organization's funds for personal items begins with petty expenditures and ends in grand larceny. If we fail to challenge small violations of values it becomes increasingly difficult to avoid the "slippery slope" of accelerating moral decline. When abuse of power becomes a way of life, our chances of correcting this, or even surviving an attempt to correct it, greatly diminish.

When we have a very positive image of a leader, we may be too quick to rationalize behavior that doesn't conform to that image. If a leader proves strategically brilliant, we can get so enamored of this brilliance that we overlook small breaches of values. If we experience discomfort with a leader's actions, we must allow ourselves to experience it, not push the feelings away because they don't conform to our images.

It is essential to challenge abuse of power early:

> **The first time the courageous follower encounters behavior antipathetic to the organization's values is the most important time to challenge the behavior, before it becomes a habit.**

> **The challenge must be skillful and completely firm; an irresolute challenge will appear to sanction the behavior.**

> **If the follower firmly and appropriately challenges the behavior, her courage and integrity will generate respect, and the leader will be prone to listen to her in the future.**

> **If the follower waits too long to challenge the leader's behavior, both the behavior and justification for it will harden, and the follower may be viewed as a nuisance or threat.**

When abuse is already entrenched, each new person who enters the leader-follower relationship has an opportunity to change the entrenched condition or be changed by it. The task is harder when abuse is entrenched, in some cases it may be dangerous, but a courageous follower can make a difference if she conveys concern and support in her challenge:

> **"As the new person here, I've been able to see things from an outsider's perspective. I think it's important you understand how things look from that perspective."**

> "I've observed practices that seem to have become accepted but will cause you trouble if not corrected."

> "You brought me in to deal with problems you were having with the organization. In addressing them, I've discovered deeper issues that may make you uncomfortable but are important for you to hear."

The road to integrity is paved with speaking up about and acting on small corruptions of principles as we encounter them; left unchecked, these moral potholes can become sinkholes that swallow the common purpose.

CHALLENGING THE USE OF LANGUAGE

Courageous followers are alert to the language of leaders as well as to their deeds. Language both shapes and reveals the beliefs underlying deeds. Pejorative words thrown about are predictive of the stones that may follow.

The use of derogatory terms to describe groups or individuals dehumanizes them and establishes the climate for abusive actions. The use of the words *yid, nigger, fag,* or *slut* have all preceded lynchings, beatings, or rapes. Their public use is now considered outrageous, but their private use continues. Even mildly diminishing language creates an "us" and "them" mentality that justifies abuse.

It requires as much courage to confront a leader about language as about behavior; it is easy for the leader to ridicule our concern and claim the words were "unimportant" or "harmless." They are not. Confronting the leader about demeaning language is a critical opportunity for establishing a relationship of principled creative challenge. It is a variation of challenging abuse early.

When leaders use euphemisms such as *collateral damage, relocation centers* or *downsizing*, we should challenge them to explore their underlying discomfort with a subject. Challenging a leader's use of language can flush value conflicts to the surface where they can be examined. Even syntax is deserving of challenge when it obscures responsibility for actions:

> "It's regrettable this happened" instead of "I'm sorry I did that."

> "Our policy has always been . . ." instead of "I support the policy."

"The budget didn't permit . . ." instead of "We cut your request."

"Civilians were killed in the bombing" instead of "Our bombing killed civilians."

We don't have to bludgeon leaders about their use of language. We can point out quietly what we just heard and our discomfort with it. Patterns of speech are so deeply ingrained that the leader may be unaware of how he used the words. We are providing the leader an opportunity to become aware of the language influencing his thoughts, masking his feelings, or coloring the messages he is sending.

History is papered over with language that obfuscates the abuse of power. By challenging leaders and groups to assume responsibility for their actions and the words they use to sanitize those actions, a courageous follower holds up a mirror that demands self-examination.

ARROGANCE

There are various attitudes and behaviors specific to individual leaders that, if present, need challenging. Arrogance is high on this list. Arrogant leadership is toxic to an organization. It looks like strength but is a debilitating weakness. If you have ever worked with an arrogant leader, you know what a low level of tolerance and respect this type has for others. Arrogant leaders make the fundamental error of believing they are qualitatively different from their followers. Failing to perceive their commonality, they lack the spiritual requirement for a life of service. Instead, they build their careers on manipulation.

A courageous follower who is working closely with an arrogant leader must try to contain the effects of the leader's behavior, as difficult as this is to do. Arrogant leaders often denigrate supporters to each other, creating an environment in which no one knows where they stand and everyone is trying to curry favor. We may be tempted to collude with this denigration if it confirms our position as part of the inner circle. But we must realize that the denigration will soon be turned against the inner circle itself if it hasn't already.

We might attempt a containment strategy along these lines:

Get the leader's agreement that it would be good to build a stronger team; from his feeling of superiority, the leader will probably agree he needs a stronger team.

Get the leader's agreement that denigrating each other weakens the team.

Then exact a simple, but critical, commitment from the leader: that he will not demean team members to each other.

By curtailing demeaning comments, the whole atmosphere surrounding the leader can change. The fires of arrogance are not continuously being stoked.

Once we have an agreement, we can challenge the leader to honor it by expressing our discomfort with the denigration when it occurs:

"_____'s not here to clarify her actions, so why don't we hold off discussing that?"

"That may not hold up under closer scrutiny. Let me investigate and report back on that."

"I'm not comfortable impugning their intentions. Let's focus on what we need from them."

"We've agreed not to harp on our own people's shortcomings. What is our responsibility as senior management for the performance problems?"

This is an instance in which, by changing behavior, we can sometimes change the underlying attitudes. In the interest of the common purpose, it is worth trying.

LEADERS WHO SCREAM

Another behavior that must be challenged is chronic screaming by a leader. Explosive anger is intimidating and tears the fabric of relationships. Things get done, but at a very heavy price. The virtue in leaders who scream is their passion for the cause and their desire to shake up people

104 THE COURAGEOUS FOLLOWER

who serve it complacently. Followers understand this. It is partly why they stay with strong leaders despite the extreme unpleasantness of the screaming behavior. Frequent angry outbursts, however, weaken both the self-esteem of followers and their bond with the leader. Abusive upbraiding is antithetical to the spirit of creative challenge. Innovative teams are not built of players who cower.

Followers are usually shocked and angry at the leader's abusive behavior. They do not realize that once a screaming pattern is established it may no longer be under the leader's conscious control. The leader is often inwardly as dismayed by the outbursts as are the followers. It is true the leader is using anger to get his way, but he is not necessarily in control of the anger. Leaders may justify their rage in the name of the cause, but it is not justified. It is just out of control.

Therefore, we should not allow new leaders to develop screaming patterns, but should challenge this behavior the first time it occurs. The norms preventing screaming loosen when one becomes the leader. The real and imagined pressures increase. This is a fertile mix for a screaming pattern to take hold unless it is immediately checked. If the leader is already established, but the follower is new to her position, she should follow the same rule and nip the behavior in the bud the first time it is directed at her.

The challenge for the follower is to maintain balance, not freeze, and not let the tantrum run unchecked. A follower can sometimes successfully impose limits on what is occurring until the leader regains self-control. The tendency, when confronted with a screaming authority figure, is to regress to the affect of a scolded child. It is critical to remain in an adult posture. Physical bearing, eye contact, tone of voice, and language can all help achieve this.

> "[John, Mr. Brown, Sir—whatever you usually call the leader], I want to discuss this. It's clearly very important to you. But I won't discuss it like this."

> If the leader can't calm down: "Let me give you a few minutes to collect yourself, and I'll be back to address your concerns."

It is noteworthy that even renowned screamers will not display the behavior with some individuals. If a follower challenges a leader firmly to treat her with respect, she may prevent an abusive pattern from taking hold in relation to herself. If the leader continues to scream at others, the courageous follower can use her own firm stand against screaming to help the leader contain his dysfunctional behavior. The follower who is not the immediate target of abuse is psychologically in a stronger position to respond.

If present when the leader explodes at a more junior person, a courageous follower can choose how to intervene. Here are some possibilities:

> **Make a firm statement and physically remove the abused person:** "Excuse me. These are serious accusations. Let me establish the precise facts of what happened with _____ and get back to you in a few minutes. Please excuse us while we talk in the next room."

> **Ask to speak with the leader privately, then and there.** Once in private, confront the leader about the behavior: "You clearly have reason to be upset. But dealing with it this way is hurting you and the organization."

Intervening in these ways interrupts the destructive pattern and allows the leader to absorb the fact that the behavior is unacceptable in the eyes of third parties. In some cases, challenging the behavior will have a calming effect, and the leader may stop displaying the behavior as frequently. In other cases, the leader may need additional help to regain control of, and transform, these excessive reactions, a case that we will examine in the next chapter.

Nearly everyone has worked at some time with a screamer. There are still plenty of screamers around but, like cigarette and cigar smoking, it is becoming much less acceptable. Fewer workplaces tolerate it, and those that do lose access to talented recruits who hear the negative word of mouth through their networks and pass on the "opportunity." In addition, like the health risks of secondhand smoke, it is attracting the lawsuits one can expect in our litigious society. There are ways to get the job done that are healthier for everyone than screaming.

PERSONAL ISSUES

We may experience acute discomfort about challenging leaders when destructive behavior occurs in their personal lives. But distinctions between personal and public life are not very useful when behavior violates the values of the organization and the society in which the organization operates. It is our responsibility to challenge the leader's behavior if it threatens to undermine trust and the common purpose.

Personal issues are the most sensitive issues on which to challenge a leader. Financial irregularities, infidelities, sexual harassment, and substance abuse are all highly emotive. The leader's response may be sharp and to the effect that we are out of line. We must be prepared to stand our ground:

> **"This is not something I would ordinarily raise, but I believe the organization's goals and your position are at risk if it is not addressed."**

> **"I know you would like to see this kept a private matter, but it is already being talked about widely, and we need to talk about it, too."**

> **"I'm not any more comfortable about discussing this than you are, but everything we are working for is being jeopardized."**

> **"If this were to appear on the front page of the Times, you and our organization would be devastated. Let's discuss it before that happens."**

We may feel outraged and betrayed by the leader's behavior, as we would if we discovered a family member doing something intensely destructive to himself or the family. When highly sensitive issues threaten to derail the leader and the organization, we need to convey how deeply we feel without attacking the leader and closing him off from our help.

NEWLY ELEVATED LEADERS

At different stages in their careers, leaders are prone to different behaviors that courageous followers may need to challenge. Leaders who are new to their positions naturally require special help from followers who have been with the organization longer and understand its nuances. Sometimes, however, a special phenomenon can occur that requires both support and challenge early on.

When leaders are suddenly elevated—promoted, appointed, or elected to senior positions—an abrupt change can take place. They are transported into another reality in which they believe they should act and be treated differently. As newly elevated leaders, they have no precedent for this experience, and they grope in the recesses of their minds for models to guide their behavior. The model they access may be real, fragmentary, or even illusory. It may be their perception, accurate or not, of how other senior leaders conduct themselves—even leaders with whom they have worked and whose leadership styles they didn't like. In extreme cases, the model they access may be an image of how a historical figure behaved in an extraordinary situation that was extremely different from the new leader's current situation. But lacking a more reality-based model, they may unconsciously base their behavior on faulty or inappropriate models.

One newly elected member of the U.S. Congress, for example, was behaving abrasively to his staff. When challenged about this behavior in a leadership development program, he became aware that he was acting like one of his party's giants who had been in Congress for several decades. Or at least, he was acting like he thought that national figure acted in his office.

Using inappropriate behavior models can create an unsettling atmosphere in which new leaders appear to suddenly change and begin acting very differently, often autocratically. They may become distant even from those who helped them achieve the new position. Power seems to have "gone to their head."

If this occurs, and we have standing with the leader as a supporter or former peer, we need to engage the leader in dialogue as early as possible about whom he is using as a role model:

"How do you see your new role?"

"How are you adjusting your style to fill that role? What are you basing that on?"

"Who are your role models? What do you admire about their leadership styles?"

"What about those styles fits the situation you find here? What differences do you see in the current situation?"

"What reactions have you been getting from others?"

"May I share some of my own reactions—the reactions I am hearing about?"

While discussing role models, the leader can examine the appropriateness and observe the consequences of his actions. Then the leader can begin to fill the new role appropriately and serve the common purpose well.

LEADERS WHO HAVE OTHER AGENDAS

New leaders can bring other agendas to their position. Old leaders can develop new agendas while in their position. Other agendas are not in themselves bad; they may even be helpful. If other agendas motivate leaders to excel in their current work, thus positioning them to achieve future goals, these other agendas indirectly serve the organization. If leaders are active in other organizations that bind them to the community, the organization may again benefit.

Sometimes other agendas don't help the organization, but they don't particularly hurt it, either. Life is full of things to do and people are fascinating mosaics of interests and motivations. A leader excessively involved with other agendas, however, can serve an organization badly. For example:

Competing agendas can distract a leader from the organization's needs, such as when a CEO devotes excessive time to serving on other boards and making outside speeches.

A leader can misuse the organization's resources for personal projects with which he is absorbed, such as writing a memoir or running for political office.

A leader's preoccupation with an agenda, such as expanding his empire through acquisitions, can squander the resources an organization has, by diverting energy from its primary purpose.

> If a leader's other agenda is hidden, such as a government official ingratiating himself with a company he would like to work for after retirement, the common purpose can be compromised.

Courageous followers who see leaders pursuing other agendas at the expense of the common purpose will challenge them as soon as their behavior becomes suspect. It may be that the leader is more motivated by the other agenda and should make preparations for a transfer of leadership so he can cleanly pursue the new purpose. Or it may be that the courageous challenge refocuses the leader on giving the common purpose the energy it requires.

LEADERS WHO WON'T CHALLENGE THEIR LEADERS

One of the most vexing and common problems for followers is finding themselves working for someone who should, but will not, challenge his or her own leader. If a leader two or more levels up from a follower is exerting unrealistic pressure on an organization, pursuing unworkable objectives, ignoring golden opportunities to advance the organization's mission, or engaging in ethically dubious activities, what does a courageous follower do?

Typically, followers in this situation bring the issue to the attention of the leader to whom they report. Unfortunately, too often it is equally typical to get weak assurances that their leader will "look into it" or "take it up at their next meeting." Often, on subsequent inquiry, followers find that these conversations didn't take place or were blown off without any real confrontation or resolution.

This poses a dilemma for a courageous follower: should this issue be pursued further and, if so, in what way? There are almost always cultural prohibitions against bypassing a direct superior to take up a matter of import with that person's superior. What are the options in this situation for a courageous follower?

The first dynamic to examine is that between the follower and her immediate leader. The follower has raised the issue with the leader, and the leader has not effectively addressed it at the higher organization level. The follower may be reluctant to raise it again for fear of becoming a nag or out of despair that raising the issue again will not do any good. It is precisely at this point that true courageous followership is needed.

If the follower considers the issue significant, she must be willing to raise it again with the leader. She may need to convey more clearly how seriously she views the issue, coach the leader on how to effectively raise it at the next level, or convey her own sense of moral responsibility to act if her leader will not do so. Some combination of statements such as these may be needed to engage the leader in dialogue that results in action:

> "I understand how sensitive this matter is, but I feel it must be addressed for the following reasons: _____."

> "If you feel I am placing undue importance on this issue, you will need to explain this to me further before I'm prepared to let it go."

> "In our previous meeting you agreed to raise the issue. I'd like to help you work through a strategy for doing so."

> "If you would prefer that I accompany you to this meeting to raise the issue, I am certainly prepared to do so."

> "If you would prefer that I directly raise this issue myself, please let me know."

> "With all due respect, this isn't the first time you have avoided raising this type of issue with _____ . If you don't raise it now, I am afraid you will be dealing with the following consequences: _____."

> "I respect you too much to go behind your back on this matter, so I am letting you know what I intend to do directly if you choose not to act further."

The central point here is that courageous followers do not absolve themselves of responsibility for potentially damaging actions occurring at a higher level of the organization simply by reporting these to their immediate superior. They engage that superior as they would any leader whom they feel is making a significant error in judgment.

If these further attempts to generate effective action fail, the follower must make the choice of what action to take. There may be other institutionalized recourses. In any case, factors of organizational culture rarely outweigh service to the common purpose and core values of the group. Purpose and values are always senior to structure. Courageous followers must sometimes directly engage leaders at higher levels of the organization to challenge behaviors or policy that threaten the organization itself. When necessary, the willingness to do so is integral to the spirit of courageous followership.

CHALLENGE YOURSELF, TOO

Creatively challenging another is a delicate act that must itself be uncorrupted. In relationships, we are prone to find fault with the other before examining ourselves, and the leader-follower relationship is no exception.

Both the leader and follower who blame the other for disappointments must look inward to find their own points of responsibility. When these are identified, understood, and owned, we can more meaningfully help each other examine our respective roles and performance.

Before challenging a leader, we should ask ourselves these questions:

> How objective am I being? Do I have my own ego-investment in this issue?

> Is "the complaint" one that I've had with other leaders, and more probably a function of my own patterns than the leader's?

> Have I had excessive expectations of the leader, which are now causing me to be excessively critical?

> Is this truly an important issue, or one in which my own sensibilities may be exaggerated?

> Am I finding fault in the leader's strategy without doing the hard work of developing alternatives for consideration?

Do I have a personal agenda that I must disclose so I do not break faith with the leader's trust in my counsel?

It is always more difficult to see ourselves clearly than to see others. If we feel on unsure ground, if we sense something familiar about our reaction, it may be wise to use someone else as a sounding board before we challenge the leader. Courage in relationships starts with an honest examination of ourselves.

5

THE COURAGE TO PARTICIPATE IN TRANSFORMATION

I FIND IT TRAGIC THAT ABLE LEADERS who fall dramatically from grace often share a common experience: their closest followers have long been aware of their fatal flaw and were unsuccessful in getting the leader to deal with it. Revelation of the flaw often comes as an unexpected shock to the broader group because it has been carefully managed and kept from public view. But those closest to the leader have usually spent long hours dealing with the fallout from the leader's behavior and discussing among themselves what to do about it.

In the political world, when a leader self-destructs, it is front-page news, so it has been easier to see examples of this behavior historically than in the business world. Every generation has its political leaders who are shamed out of office, soundly defeated at the polls, or worse. Most are soon forgotten even by their own generation, but a few flame out spectacularly and become part of the national lore, at least for a while.

In the United States, former civil rights activist and Washington, DC, mayor Marion Barry's cocaine habit and late-night hotel rendezvousing ended in a sting operation, jail sentence, and international disgrace for the Capitol City. President Richard Nixon's paranoia led him to encourage and cover up the dirty tricks that took the nation to the brink of constitutional crisis and eventually forced his resignation. He only eluded criminal prosecution by a presidential pardon from his successor. President Bill Clinton's lifelong pattern of wriggling out of the consequences of personally and politically risky behavior played into the hands of his political enemies when he emphatically and falsely denied an involvement with government intern Monica Lewinsky. This experience nearly cost him the presidency, certainly damaged his reputation, and contributed to his party losing the White House in the subsequent election.

More recently, we have begun to see public exposure of similar phenomena in other areas of leadership, including the church, business, finance, and government agencies. What a terrible waste to lose a leader's talents because of one undesirable pattern of behavior! In nearly every case, there were undoubtedly individuals who tried to confront these leaders about their behavior and were ignored, refuted, given unkept promises, or shunted out of the inner circle. But the fact that they tried tells us that the courage to challenge isn't itself always sufficient.

Behavior that flagrantly violates values may be symptomatic of a deeply ingrained psychological pattern or an addiction, which takes more than a request to change. We can't tell leaders something once and then abandon our accountability for the impact of their behavior on our common purpose. Challenging something once does not give us the right to lean back cynically and say, "Well, they never listen!" We must search for approaches that reach our leaders and methods to help them transform the damaging behavior.

This requires courage for several reasons. First, we have to admit to ourselves how serious the situation actually is, how gravely it endangers the organization's work. Second, we may have to examine our own collusion with the leader's behavior, what we do that allows it to continue. Third, transformation is an inexact activity and can easily fail, leaving us the discredited champions of a very lost cause.

Some people don't believe transformation is even possible. Our culture tells us "You can't teach an old dog new tricks." I had one foundation reject a proposal I had written to fund an ethics workshop for members of the U.S. Congress and their staffs because "the individual's moral character is formed by early adulthood and can't thereafter be changed."

The attitude that people can't change is defeatist. I want to vigorously challenge that thinking in relation to leaders and followers. I can't responsibly write about challenging leaders and taking moral stands without also writing about transforming. That option must be explored. It's easy to write someone off. It's also lazy and wasteful to do so if it can be avoided.

I believe that one of the most important advances of the closing decades of the last millennium was the increasing use of transformative techniques, as imperfect as they may be. This may turn out to be one of the lasting contributions of the controversial sixties generation with its emphasis on human potential and development. For example, we see widespread acceptance of twelve-step programs for a range of addictions. We have become compassionate and sophisticated about helping war veterans and disaster victims process their trauma. Marriage counseling and family therapy are more frequently used today as options to slow the alarming divorce rate generated by the sexual and social revolution of the sixties and seventies.

At the same time that we see an increased use of transformation techniques, we see many failures in transformation attempts: the family member who keeps reverting to drugs, the war veteran who commits suicide, the marriage that fails despite counseling. Even more disturbing are the things about ourselves we would like to change but have never been successful at changing. These make it hard for us to believe in transformation.

It is true that personal transformation is extremely difficult, often the most difficult challenge of our lives. I believe that we must, nevertheless, open up to its possibilities. If a behavior threatens to overwhelm our larger purpose, we must find the skilled help to support a transformation effort, muster the courage to pursue it, and exert the discipline required to achieve transformation. Transformation efforts should be attempted when a practice or behavior that violates the organization's values and threatens its purpose is so entrenched that it is barely understood to be a legitimate problem, let alone one of potentially catastrophic dimensions.

Often strong internal and external pressures are working against a leader's transformation. I have personally experienced some of these pressures. At one time I had a deserved reputation for being a screamer who used threatening behavior to get things done. I didn't like my out-of-control anger; it obviously hurt people and depressed morale. But I used my track record of turning around poorly performing offices to justify it. The behavior served me well in a high-pressured, results-now environment. Though I was ashamed of how out-of-control the behavior was, I was defensive when anyone intimated it was wrong.

Eventually, the behavior caused enough serious problems in my professional and personal lives, and enough discordance with my basic value system, that I achieved some success in modifying it. But when organizational performance lagged, headquarters questioned whether I was going soft! It was only after leaving this culture and joining a different organization, which wouldn't tolerate abusive behavior and presented me with other models of success, that I was able to truly transform it in my professional life.

Although this chapter will focus on personal behavior requiring transformation, it is also true that sometimes the need for personal and organizational transformation is intertwined. Characteristics of one reinforce the other. For example, a leader in a corporate setting with a strong vision and a persuasive personality will be likely to attract shareholders, directors, and senior staff who desire to benefit from the success the leader generates. Expectations skyrocket, and handsome rewards are built into the system to encourage achieving lofty financial goals. As this organization appears to become more and more successful, there is less and less questioning of the methods being used to achieve success. A "don't look a gift horse in the mouth" attitude develops. Whatever flaw the particular leader of the operation may have—grandiosity, poor ability to integrate acquired operations, lack of concern for legal niceties—is overlooked by the system and is often rewarded and reinforced. This removes all apparent incentive for transformation and worsens the risk that the leader will continue behaving in deeply problematic ways. For transformation to occur, both the leader and the system need to be engaged in the effort.

Similarly, an organization may desperately need to move from a centralized command-and-control culture to a decentralized, risk-taking, service-oriented environment. But the organization can't effectively make this change until its leaders deal with their own exaggerated control needs. Transformation needs to be stimulated in both dimensions.

The transformation can be goal oriented or process oriented—for example, to clean up the impact the organization's practices are having on the environment or to improve the way its leaders involve others in decision making. Sometimes, it can be both.

Too often, leaders do not become sufficiently motivated to engage in the tough job of changing their behavior until they have lived through a crisis precipitated by the behavior. By then the damage is usually extensive. Some people believe the motivation for transformation can't be developed short of a crisis. It is my view that the role of courageous followers is to preempt that crisis by engaging the leader in transformation before the storm.

When dealing with a hard-bitten leader, the prospect of transformation may seem hopeless; the leader may seem unapproachable on the subject and our efforts may cause a backlash and worsen the situation. The leader may be surrounded with advisers who have a strong vested interest in the leader not changing the status quo that is lining their pockets. They may attack the follower who is championing change. But there are times when transformation must be attempted by a courageous follower, despite the risks. When we have a purpose we believe in and a strong, committed leader, it is worth all the effort to transform potentially tragic flaws. Ask hard-bitten leaders who have been derailed by their flaws if, in retrospect, they don't wish their followers had tried harder to get through to them.

When the transformation needed involves not just the leader's own behavior but also fundamental parts of the system, courageous followers will need to be extremely skillful in finding organizational support for their efforts and presenting compelling evidence to make their case. They will need to be particularly adroit in describing the potential consequences in terms that convey the pain of failing to transform as greater than the pain of transforming, where they believe this to be true.

This chapter focuses primarily on helping a leader with the process of personal transformation. It is based on my own observations and reflections, on my personal transformation efforts, and on the few studies that have been done by others attempting to help senior executives change. I don't pretend to present a definitive approach to transformation for leaders or followers. Extensive dialogue and investigation is needed on this subject. I hope to provide some useful guidance. I begin this chapter with a statement of general principles, which the literature on human change suggests are true in any transformation effort. I also examine how resistance to change, which is present in all transformation efforts, manifests in particular in leaders. And most germanely, I explore what a courageous follower's role should be in a transformation effort.

It is very challenging for both leaders and followers to do the internal work necessary for transformation while keeping things going externally in their professional and personal lives. In the following pages, we will explore how the process might work.

WHEN IS TRANSFORMATION POSSIBLE?

Consciousness of the need for transformation can occur when leaders have gradually prepared for change and are ready to embrace it, or when they are unprepared for it and life events force them to wake up.

Usually, multiple life events contribute to an individual's or group's readiness for transformation. For example, a leader may be aware that her industry is going through profound changes, the exact shape of which won't be clear for years. At the same time, she may have attended a conference at which she heard another leader describe experiences preparing an organization to deal with these changes. And she may have had a taste of the power of transformative interventions at a leadership development program she attended. The combination of these events sparked commitment to change, to exploring new visions of what she and the organization could become.

Often, the combination of events that opens a leader to change, especially of a personal nature, is less positive. The organization has lost significant revenues. There have been disaffections from its senior ranks in reaction to the leader's authoritarian style. Negative press stories are further hurting morale. The stress of handling the job is having painful ramifications on the leader's personal relations. Perhaps she has developed serious physical symptoms from the stress. Too often, failure or trauma—divorce, heart attack, scandal, loss of position, prosecution—occurs before a leader opens to transformation.

The essential steps that make transformation possible are the acknowledgment of the need for change, the admission of blemish, the owning of some responsibility for the current state of affairs, and a glimpse of the potential to become something better.

THE PROCESS OF PERSONAL TRANSFORMATION

Let's examine what the process of transforming attitudes and behavior consists of, as well as the forces that can impede or facilitate the process.

SELF-ORGANIZING PROCESSES

Though many living things transform themselves, we don't expect a caterpillar to become an eagle, a tadpole to become a fox, or an acorn to become an apple tree. Every lifeform has its own mature potential. Similarly, we cannot expect an individual to radically change her personality, but we can expect and encourage that individual to evolve to her full potential.

Each human being has a core personality. That personality is formed and held in place, at least in part, by certain "core ordering" processes. These include how we organize experience into our view of reality, how we form our sense of identity, how we rank our values, and how we try to control our environment. Because these processes form the core of "who we are," they are very durable and not easily subject to change. They make us recognizable to our college classmates at our twentieth reunion, and to ourselves as we pass through the stages of our lives. But they are not immutable.

DISCOMFORT, THREAT, AND CRISIS

Human beings generally maintain a dynamic state of balance until faced with a dramatically new situation in the form of a novel opportunity, a unique challenge, or a crisis. Then either we accommodate to these events and achieve a new dynamic balance, or our framework for life begins to unravel.

When we experience too much threat to our core ordering processes, we try even harder to use our old solutions. If these fail, we may experience a "breakdown"—physical, emotional, mental. The pain of the breakdown serves the function of demanding that we pay attention to our need to change.

RESISTANCE

It is completely usual to resist change even when we see change is desirable or necessary. We are fearful that we will lose important parts of ourselves that have made our lives work up to now. We can respect this resistance and its self-protecting purpose without succumbing to it. We can allow it to modulate the pace of change to a rate we can tolerate, without letting it sentence us to stagnation. We will find ourselves alternately opening and closing to the prospect of change. If we honor these natural fluctuations, we can use them to enter and retreat from new territory until we have surveyed it, chosen our preferred positions, and incorporated them into our core processes.

DEVELOPING UNDERSTANDING

As we open to the need for change, we observe more about our relationship to ourselves and our relationships to others. We observe how we feel and what we do in a particular situation; and we observe the consequences of these feelings and actions.

Observation is the first step in reengineering a process. We need to know exactly what the current process is and exactly what needs it serves. Then we can consider how to change it, how to get legitimate needs met more efficiently and thoroughly. We must understand our current patterns, their depth and force, and how much we rely on them. Then we can do the hard work of transforming them.

WILLINGNESS TO EXPERIMENT

As we open to transformation, we realize that the way we have done things, which seemed to be the only way things could or should be done, is not in fact the only way. And it may not be the best way. We begin to explore the options open to us.

We may try doing the opposite of our ingrained response, testing what it feels like to use nonhabitual behavior. We may let our recessive traits come to the fore and see what effect they have. It can be a small behavior we do differently, like listening at a meeting rather than jumping in early with forcefully made arguments.

Usually, the sustainable options open to us are not those at the other end of the spectrum. They may be a few degrees further in the direction we would like to go. We may place a little more value on something we previously ignored and a little less value on something we previously held sacrosanct—for example, a little less value on a deadline and a little more

value on the impact of the deadline on ourselves and our family. We experiment and evaluate the results.

INTEGRATION

We cannot form a clear vision of realistic and desirable outcomes before
we begin a transformation process. Transformation takes us from the
known to the unknown. As the process unfolds, we begin to envision new,
desirable states. Often they are more complex than we could articulate at
the outset, involving the integration of different factors—the hard and
soft, the dark and light sides of our personality. When we can visualize a
realistic outcome we can use it to guide and measure our progress. We can
refocus from what was "wrong" to what we are becoming

The process of personal transformation moves from disorienting,
threatening beginnings, to sobering and eye-opening middles, to invig-
orating and rejuvenating outcomes. It requires courage to stay with this
volatile process.

THE FOLLOWER'S ROLE

In all situations calling for transformation, the people closest to the individual in need of change play a pivotal role. Our primary relationships are
the arena in which transformation of attitude and behavior is most likely
to occur. As followers who are close to a leader, we have the power to play
that pivotal role:

> We can complicitly deny the need for transformation and cover
> it up, or we can openly contrast existing behaviors against desir-
> able behaviors.

> We can tolerate abusive or dysfunctional behavior, or we can
> draw a line in the sand.

> We can fall in step with disruptive behavior, or we can model
> functional ways of interacting.

> We can judge and rail against leaders' failings, or we can see some
> of their struggles in ourselves.

> We can create a hostile environment in which leaders fight for
> their lives, or we can provide the support they need to experi-
> ment and learn about personal change.

The paradox of transformation, from the follower's perspective, is that
it cannot be achieved by focusing solely on the leader. Such a focus can
become obsessive and manipulative. If we wish to help a leader transform,
we must ourselves be willing to participate in the process of transformation. We need to examine our own role in the relationship with the leader.
That is the only role we potentially have full power to change. We need
to notice what we do that enables and colludes with a leader's dysfunctional behavior. For example, do we cower each time the leader throws a
tantrum and then frantically execute her barked orders? This reinforces
the leader's experience that tantrums are the way to control the environment. If we change that part of ourselves, the leader may make adjustments
to find a new fit with us.

Although the balance of the chapter will discuss how a courageous follower supports a leader's transformation efforts, followers may want to seek
similar support for their own transformation efforts.

THE FOLLOWER AS CATALYST

The task of courageous followers who see life's harsh wake-up call coming is to effectively make a leader aware of the need to preempt that call.
This is often much harder than it sounds. Anyone engaging in dysfunctional behavior has a lot of defenses built up around it and a lot of filters
in place to screen out messages that disconfirm their behavior.

How do we get leaders' own alarm bells ringing? How do we provide
a simulator in which they can experience potential disaster without actually going through the crash that will damage both themselves and, very
likely, those they should be serving? Courageous followers can become
both amplifiers and interpreters of the events they want a leader to pay
attention to.

Though leaders are probably aware, to some degree, of their problematic behavior, motivation to transform is created only when they real-

ize how seriously others view it. This is a central point for courageous followers to comprehend:

> Because offending leaders rationalize the seriousness of their actions, they assume others will also minimize that seriousness. This is their fatal error in judgment.

> Conveying the intensity of our dismay, our concern, our outrage about the leader's practices is the single most important act courageous followers can take as catalysts for change.

If we understate our feelings out of deference to a leader's position, out of discomfort with vocalizing the truth as we see it, or out of fear of the leader's reaction, we will be ineffective as agents of change. The skill required is to deliver the message in a way that conveys our support for the leader without pulling punches. We can do this if we target the behavior, not the leader:

> "You and I share a deep commitment to the purposes of this organization. We cannot let those purposes be jeopardized by denying the serious impact _____ [dysfunctional behavior] is having on the organization."

> "Once you grasp the importance of an issue, no one is more capable of vigorously addressing it than you. I am very afraid that _____ [dysfunctional behavior] is bringing this organization to the brink of disaster."

> "If I were doing something that jeopardized my career, I know you wouldn't quietly let me drive over the cliff, and I can't let you do that, either."

> "You've led this organization brilliantly, but we can't let that obscure how these actions are violating common decency."

Transformation occurs most readily in an atmosphere of tough love—a genuine appreciation for the person and a steadfast stance against the behaviors that are detrimental to the person and the organization. We each have our issues and time for transformation, and in

healthy relationships, we take turns being a clear-eyed and resolute catalyst for the other.

CHANNELING THE
LEADER'S FRUSTRATION

Some leaders in need of serious self-examination experience frustration
with the failings of others and do not make the link to failings in themselves. Rather than this presenting a problem, it may present an opportunity to involve the leader in a transformation process.

Especially if a leader explodes or dissolves under criticism, it may be
more effective to first mirror back to the leader the difficulties she is
reporting with others before confronting her with her contribution to the
situation. Mirroring consists of paraphrasing the leader's frustration and
communicating it back to her in a way that shows she has been heard,
empathizes with her feelings, and reflects her self-image so she feels understood and appreciated. For example:

> **"I see that you are trying hard to weld together a first-class team
> that provides the best service possible. It must be extremely frus-
> trating that not all of your people seem to be getting the idea."**

Once the leader feels understood, the follower can suggest a thorough
review of the organization's systems to get at the root problems. Reviewing systems rarely seems threatening. A leader who is frustrated with a
staff's performance is often open to such a suggestion, genuinely thinking
the problems are "there," not "here."

From a systems perspective, great leadership and great followership are
part of the same system. Though leaders may not be able to meaningfully
hear that a system review will include examining their own role in the system, they need to be briefed on this for both ethical and practical reasons.
Leaders' acceptance that they *may* be involved in performance issues opens
the door to a review of their style and impact. If the leader is, indeed, a
primary cause of system dysfunction, this will emerge in the review. Followers, of course, must be prepared to discover their own contribution to
the dysfunctional system.

Whoever conducts the review will need to confront both the leader and followers about their roles in the dysfunction. The same caveat applies as was given to the follower-as-catalyst: to generate the motivation to change, the confrontation must clearly communicate the intensity of feelings within the group about the behavior and practices discovered in the review.

DENIAL AND JUSTIFICATION OF BEHAVIOR

The greatest barrier to changing dysfunctional behavior is denial or justification of the behavior. Leaders are prone to discount the importance of their destructive behavior on the grounds that up to now it hasn't prevented them from attaining success.

Often, however, the leader has been successful because of a less extreme and more functional version of this behavior, or because of another trait used in tandem with the destructive behavior. Vices and virtues are extensions of the same underlying quality. If courageous followers can help a leader distinguish between the destructive behavior and a related virtue, and can affirm the importance of the virtue, they may be able to open the leader to transformation:

> "You've always inspired people with graphic visions of a better future and shown them ways to improve their lives. What you're doing now is different because you are misrepresenting this investment as less risky than it is and endangering their future."

> "You may think it's the staff's fear of your anger that gets them to do what you want, but it's actually your determination and commitment. The anger just erodes their willingness to support you and the organization."

Hubris is that marvelous classical word that sums up the danger to those who have experienced success. It is defined as "insolence or arrogance resulting from excessive pride." It can be lethal to the leader and the common purpose.

History and the daily newspaper are strewn with examples of hubris brought to its knees, of successful lives ruined by self-defeating behavior:

billionaires sent to jail, CEOs ousted by boardroom rebellions, national figures tarred by prejudices that slip out in public speech, labor leaders pilloried for misappropriating funds, celebrities dead from drug overdoses. We may need to remind the leader of such stories in painful detail. Each form of hubris has its examples, its warnings for others. The individuals in these examples were also once in exalted positions, too successful to heed warnings up until the moment of their downfall.

If ever courage is called for, it is when followers need to confront supremely confident leaders who are at the pinnacle of their careers, and tell them that their hundred-foot yachts are about to run into reefs and sink unless they make a radical change in course. If successful leaders are fortunate, they will have courageous followers in their crew.

DEDICATION TO CAUSE
AS JUSTIFICATION

Leaders sometimes use their dedication to the cause to justify inappropriate behavior, and then they construe a challenge to their behavior as an attack on the cause. Leaders may come to consider their own welfare so critical to the success of the organization that they justify anything they do for themselves, regardless of its appropriateness, on the grounds that it enables them to better serve the organization. Financial improprieties and misuse of the organization's resources are particularly prone to this type of justification.

Failure to maintain the boundary between the self and the organization or cause is one of the most dangerous confusions of identity a leader can experience. This is especially true when the leader is the founder of the organization, and the group itself confuses the identities of the leader and the organization. A courageous follower can approach this situation in several ways:

> At a functional level, we must try to help the leader see the consequences of her behavior and how it is hurting the very cause that represents her life's work.

> At a deeper level, we can try to help the leader identify her underlying needs and find ways of satisfying these that are more appropriate than her existing behavior.

> At the most profound level, we may need to encourage the leader to reclaim her own identity and separate it from the organization or cause.

Sometimes a leader's identity is so completely immersed in the organization or cause that transformation is not possible; you cannot change something that you cannot find. In this situation, the leader must reclaim some of her independent identity as a prerequisite to change. A radical shift of environment, activity, power relationships, and focus, even for just a month, may create the fresh perspective needed. Here are some examples of opportunities for a leader to take a break that will help reestablish her boundaries with the organization:

> A senior executive program at a prestigious university or one of the better, transformation-oriented leadership development institutions

> An extended family vacation, far from the seat of her power, at the urging of family and friends

> An appointment to a demanding public service position that engages the leader differently for a period

> A sabbatical to write, research, or rejuvenate

> A spiritual retreat at a center maintained for these purposes by the leader's religious denomination, or at one of a growing number of nondenominational spiritual retreat facilities

> A residential rehabilitation facility if substance dependency has entered the picture

Sometimes senior executives arrange these breaks for themselves by having heart attacks or other life-threatening problems that motivate them to review their values and open themselves to transformation. Courageous followers provide gentler alternatives for leaders to step back and reclaim important parts of themselves.

REACTIONS TO CONFRONTATION

The act of inviting a leader to join in a transformation process itself initiates change. Raising an issue with a leader ensures that things will never be quite the same, even if the change produced is subtle, and whether or not the change is positive from your perspective. We really do live in the universe described by quantum physics, in which even the act of bearing witness to an event changes that event.

When we invite leaders to join in a transformation process, we are probably going to generate some confusion and discomfort. They may wonder:

> "What exactly are these people asking of me?"

> "Don't they think well of me?"

> "What are their motives?"

> "Is there danger in this?"

> "How far am I willing to go with it?"

> "Is this really necessary?"

We must be willing to make the leader uncomfortable when we challenge her behavior. She may experience anger at being confronted, or depression because her positive self-image is being called into question. These are often necessary stages before acceptance can occur. We must be willing to deal with the leader's reaction, and the discomfort that may cause us, if we are to form an effective transformative relationship.

For transformation to occur, relationship rules need to change. We cannot relate at a superficial level. We need to be open and take risks. We can't ask a leader to transform dysfunctional behavior and hide it at the same time. When we invite a leader into a transformative process, we must be prepared to see what's under the visible part of the iceberg, to experience that, too. We need to do this as compassionate adults who have power and choice in the relationship, who are asking to see the whole person, not as children who only want to see our parents' nurturing side.

If leaders vehemently disagree with our assessments, it doesn't mean we have failed. We may have started a process in which the leader asks, "Why am I getting these reactions from people?" Confronting leaders does not mean insisting that they see what we see about them. We may perceive part of the picture, or perceive it with partial accuracy. Others will perceive different parts, as in the parable of the blind men who each describe only the part of the elephant they can feel.

We can't let a leader off the hook about what we perceive. We may need to press our point hard, but only until the leader starts to get the message that something about her behavior is amiss and needs attention. At that point we must respect the leader's ability to identify the parts of the problem that her core ordering processes will allow her to begin addressing.

Raising consciousness means getting leaders to see what *they* can see, to expand their perception so they see more than they do now, so they get a sense of their blind spots. We can tell leaders what we see, but this is just a starting point to get their attention. The task is to get them looking in a direction they would rather not look, to awaken their interest in doing so, to get their own considerable energy involved in the process.

IDENTIFYING TRANSFORMATION RESOURCES

Once we have the attention of a leader and have interested her in transforming her behavior or practices, we should be prepared to suggest vehicles for doing so. While some of the process of transformation can be done on our own, most people find it requires support from others or professional guidance. We will probably encourage a planned intervention, a selected set of actions that will help the leader and the group move toward desired outcomes. The approach we recommend will grow out of the conditions we are trying to address:

> If the issue involves group dynamics, such as a nonparticipatory, autocratic decision-making style, an intervention is needed that addresses team processes.

> If the issue is personal, such as substance abuse, then individual counseling, rehabilitation, and a support group are indicated.

> If the issue concerns abuse of power, such as the questionable use of funds, an intervention will need to establish external controls as well as address internal psychological issues.

Often a combination of interventions is needed to clarify values and vision, improve team skills and processes, and examine what underlies individual attitudes and behaviors affecting those processes.

Sometimes it is best for the leader and followers to go through a transformational intervention together.

At other times it is preferable for the leader to participate in an experiential learning process with peers from other groups.

In some cases working with real issues is preferable, while in others it is more productive to use simulations and group exercises.

Whatever permits participants to experience and name the current state, to understand the price it exacts, and to name and desire a preferred state to work toward can be a transformative vehicle.

Consulting with professionals as needed, courageous followers examine the range of intervention choices and select appropriate modalities to recommend. We have to weigh the pros and cons of different approaches. For example, if we are considering recommending professional counseling as an option, the advantages include its potential for getting to issues below the surface as well as the fact that it is privileged communication. A disadvantage may be that the confidential nature of the process makes it hard for followers to know what's happening and inappropriate to inquire.

Whatever approach is suggested, it is often helpful for the leader and other participants in the process to have a clearly assigned partner, coach, or mentor—someone who is available to provide support between formal interventions. For the leader this might be a board member, a senior member of the staff who is respected for good judgment and fairness, or a former executive of the organization. Coaches can observe the progress of the transformation process, provide a reality check on our perceptions of change, and be advocates for the leader or ourselves as we each struggle honestly, but not always successfully, to make desired changes.

USING AN OUTSIDE FACILITATOR

If a group intervention is indicated, it is advisable to use an outside facilitator unbiased by preconceptions and uninvolved with organizational politics. An outside facilitator can ask difficult questions, make difficult observations, and be trusted to respect the confidentiality of the process. Otherwise, our tough job is made even tougher. We are part of the change process. It's hard to both facilitate it and be part of it. They are different roles.

Retaining outside professional help is usually understood by the leader and accepted as a sensible approach. Occasionally a leader may object to the suggestion, saying, "What am I paying you for if we need someone else to fix this?" This is a curve ball. Organizations retain specialists all the time for special assignments: a legal department retains outside counsel, a marketing department hires advertising agencies, a personnel department uses executive search firms. Courageous followers make this case forcefully if the situation warrants outside support.

If a leader is uncomfortable with the prospect of a formal intervention, followers can help the leader overcome the discomfort:

> **Discuss the safeguards established in the process to protect the leader's self-esteem, public image, and sensibilities.**
>
> **Find peers who have been through similar processes, and encourage the leader to listen to their experiences.**
>
> **Discuss the range of possible interventions and find one with which the leader feels comfortable.**
>
> **Arrange for the leader to meet with potential facilitators of these interventions to develop familiarity and trust.**

The more leaders understand and buy into the process, the greater the chance they will be fully engaged as it unfolds. As change agents, it is the responsibility of both the follower and the facilitator to help participants, including the leader, understand and open up to the process.

Sadly, something of a cultural taboo against personal counseling persists, though counseling may be part of the optimum intervention. Particularly in public life, some people see a leader's need for therapy or counseling as calling the leader's fitness for office into question. This attitude is a terrible disservice to our leaders and ourselves. It denies our leaders tremendous growth opportunity, and it denies us the benefit of self-examined leadership. This attitude is changing, however, among some public figures who understand the value of exploring and repairing old personal or family issues that may interfere with their optimal performance.

If a leader does seek professional counseling to address the underlying causes of intractable behavior, it should be construed as a sign of strength, not weakness, and should be fully supported and defended by courageous followers.

CREATING A SUPPORTIVE ENVIRONMENT

Transformation requires a secure vessel—the equivalent of a protective cocoon in which the work can be done. This is difficult to create in the hurly-burly world of fast-moving organizations. It can be done, however, by followers who are committed to creating a caring community.

We sometimes hear of the loneliness at the top of an organization. Leaders do often feel alone, though sometimes the aloneness is of their own making. We need to communicate that they are not alone in their transformation efforts. We will support them and stand by them. We will share responsibility for the progress of the transformation effort with them.

Sooner or later, whatever the method used to become aware of existing behavior patterns and their impact, the leader needs to experiment with changing these patterns. Experimentation requires a supportive environment. Trying different ways of doing things will initially feel awkward or unnatural. We don't know what is going to happen when we experiment. It's okay to fall off the bike when we're learning to ride, as long as we won't get laughed at. Or run over. Experiments produce both excitement and anxiety.

How do courageous followers create a supportive environment in which leaders can move through a transformation process? Here are some guidelines:

> **Let leaders know we see their willingness to take on the challenge of transformation as a sign of their strength as a leader.**

> **Continue to communicate clearly about the impact of their behavior; sustain the external pressure that requires them to generate enough internal pressure to avoid deflation of the transformation effort.**

> Show patience: remember the strength of the forces that tenaciously hold existing behavior patterns in place.
>
> Continue to work on our own transformation; share our struggles, as appropriate, with the leader and thus share our journeys.
>
> Create an environment clearly supportive of the leader's new behaviors by providing the complementary behaviors required for the leader's efforts to be successful.

We should encourage leaders to share their efforts at changing their behavior with those affected by their behavior. Leaders should acknowledge the behavior and its effects and explain what they are trying to do about it. There may be initial cynicism about their sincerity, but if they are authentically struggling to transform, this sincerity will soon come across. Openness about the need to change generates further support.

By involving the immediate community in the transformation effort, leaders create their own additional internal commitment to implement and sustain new behaviors. Not only do leaders not want to fail after announcing their intentions, they also do not want to let down those who are being so supportive.

The individuals and groups affected by a leader's behavior must be open to the possibility of the leader changing. Too often there is a refusal to let go of past mistakes leaders have made. "I don't trust her because . . . ." Courageous followers confront the group as well as the leader. Group members need to be willing to take another chance, to proceed with cautious open-mindedness, not cynically dismiss the transformation effort before it begins or preordain its failure.

Even if we've been victimized by the leader, we need to support a genuine transformation effort. This is the heart of forgiveness—forgiving who someone once was, out of respect for whom they are trying to become.

MODELING CHANGE FOR A LEADER

When a leader is engaged in transformation, old ways of doing things become insupportable and start to break down. The leader begins searching for new ways of doing things. Models become important.

Followers can sometimes provide those models. A follower is no more a paragon of exemplary behavior than a leader, but we each have our strengths. The leader models behavior that we learn from all the time; we can do the same for the leader. The most germane behavior we can model to help a leader transform is our own openness to transformation. And our openness to transformation begins by being willing to show our vulnerabilities.

We are not prone to showing vulnerabilities around leaders, nor are they prone to doing so around us. We are selected or hired to be competent, to have or generate answers, to be part of the solution. Yet if we feel we can never appear uncertain or vulnerable, we are telling our leaders they cannot be vulnerable either. Openness sets the stage for leaders and followers to engage in a genuine change process. We need to learn and, by our example, teach that some degree of shared vulnerability is necessary for transformation.

How do we model openness to change?

We can initiate discussions of sensitive topics about ourselves.

We can model soliciting personal feedback by showing genuine interest in how others perceive us.

We can voice our fears and not duck the subject when others raise their fears.

We can talk about the negative impact our behavior has on others and how we are trying to remedy that.

We can talk about both our successes and our setbacks with our own transformation efforts.

Modeling vulnerability is a real test of courage. It's risky. It can be turned on us. It can be overdone. But the alternative is stagnation behind rigid facades that we all work overtime to maintain.

MODELING EMPATHY

We can model any characteristic we possess or develop, but the most important one to model may be empathy. A leader must be able to empathize with real people and not just serve abstractions. Among the most abusive acts are those committed by leaders who passionately pursue revolutionary social goals but are incapable of feeling or identifying with the pain of a single individual.

This anesthetized condition occurs more frequently among men. In many cultures boys are trained to repress their feelings, and they learn this lesson well. Its extreme manifestation occurs in men who gravitate to power out of a deep psychological need to deny their vulnerability. By contrasting their strength with the weakness of their victims, they stave off feeling vulnerable. Fear of feeling fear shuts down all feelings.

Because these individuals cannot experience their own feelings, they cannot identify with another's. The "other" can then be objectified and dehumanized, which sets the climate for inhumane acts to be perpetrated against them. This may not be the usual climate in which we live and work, but evidence of this condition exists all around us—in the daily news stories about rival gang gunfights, ethnic atrocities, and brutal civil wars. Someone is "leading" those acts, and others are following.

Most of the situations we encounter will fall far short of these extremes, but even in more moderate cases, it is imperative to help an "unfeeling" leader regain the ability to feel the pain of another human being. A follower's most available and powerful tool for doing this is his own feelings. It is a mistake for a follower whose leader is shut off from feelings to allow the leader to become the model for feeling behavior in the group.

Instead, a courageous follower will model for the leader how to contact feelings and will demonstrate the difference between compassion and weakness. A follower must listen carefully to his feelings about the leader's words and actions, and report those feelings to the leader as he would describe visual events to a person who has lost his sight:

"That scares me because it lacks respect for basic human rights."

"I would feel betrayed if that action were directed at me."

"I feel disappointed hearing you say that, and I think others will, too."

"My trust would be severely shaken."

"Real people will experience real pain if that occurs."

"I feel outraged hearing you discuss people in those terms."

"I would cry if I found we were party to such an action."

Leaders who lack empathy are also chronically disdainful of others. They have lost touch with the actual conditions of the lives of their followers and the lives of those whom the organization serves. Disdainful leaders no longer understand the challenges followers face in getting their jobs done. They harp on lack of perfection and undermine the mutual respect needed to pursue a common purpose.

A transformational strategy is needed to increase empathy and bridge the gulf between the disdainful leader and others. The story of the monarch who disguises himself to roam among his subjects and find out what they really think and feel is applicable. Some organizations require senior executives to spend a week or two a year doing front-line jobs so they stay connected to the reality of what it takes to serve customers. Actually doing, not inspecting or critiquing, jobs at different levels of the organization can be eye-opening as to the skill required and the problems encountered. Disdain may rapidly transform into admiration and respect, or at least understanding.

Getting out in the field and talking to the end consumer of the organization's work—the trucker who drives the vehicles the company builds, the pensioner who depends on the services the agency provides, the family who is counting on the insurance company to come through for them—helps restore the loss of empathy that success and prominence sometimes breed.

Courageous followers can encourage leaders to agree that they and their closest followers take turns occasionally doing frontline jobs. As we gain prestige in tandem with our leaders, we are also susceptible to losing our empathy for others, and must periodically close the distance that arises between us and those we serve.

CONTAINING ABUSIVE BEHAVIOR

While modeling ways to change, followers may also need to help leaders contain abusive behavior until they can transform it. For example, a leader who screams needs to modify this behavior while working to transform the underlying causes. Otherwise, the bond between the leader, followers, and common purpose is severely weakened.

Anger is a potentially creative tool if it is not repressed or allowed to get out of control. It can be used as an emotional sensor to detect something wrong that cannot yet be fully articulated. Learning to see repressed anger and invite its verbal expression can prevent the anger from reaching a boiling point where it becomes abusive.

But in leaders who display sudden, explosive anger, the emotional energy is so great that it demands physical release before the underlying situation can be verbalized and explored. A courageous follower coaching a leader in alternatives to abusive ranting might consider the following:

> Anger triggers the "fight or flight" mechanism; the adrenalin this pumps through the system must be released.
>
> In a person who slowly builds up anger, excess adrenalin can be drained by regular physical exercise; many people who work closely with leaders know what a difference exercise makes to their leaders' temperament.
>
> In leaders who become suddenly overwhelmed with anger, it is more difficult finding socially acceptable outlets for the adrenalin; behavior such as throwing things, fist banging, and hurling epithets intimidates others and is abusive.
>
> Ideally, mechanisms for releasing the anger would be used by the leader in private, but sometimes an otherwise highly regarded leader cannot exert the self-control to do this. In this case, it may help to have tools available for the leader's use when needed.
>
> Although doing so may seem strange, it is far less intimidating behavior for a leader convulsed with anger to dissipate it by twisting a golf towel or squeezing the back of an upholstered chair, while repeating a nondirective epithet such as "damn," than to verbally abuse followers. A quick walk around the block will further dampen the surge of stress hormones.
>
> In a quieter moment, the leader can explain why she is doing this; the objective is to release the physical energy without wounding people with verbal shrapnel and threatening behavior.

Efforts at transforming abuse are not a license to continue the abuse. Since abusive behavior is immature, when courageous followers set limits on what they will tolerate, it helps leaders contain the behavior. Containing abusive behavior buys leaders the time they need to explore the roots of the behavior and work through the transformation process.

POSITIVE REINFORCEMENT

Insights may occur in a flash, but this is rarely true of lasting transformation. Translating insights into new ways of relating to ourselves and others is usually a long, uneven process. Successful transformation is assisted by reinforcement when we are successful at changing a behavior and disconfirmation when we are not. Reinforcement and disconfirmation require an outside agent, and followers can perform this role for a leader. It will help to bear these principles in mind when providing reinforcement:

> **Constant correction erodes self-confidence.**
>
> **If leaders feel assaulted or harassed, they will wall themselves off from continued criticism to protect their self-esteem and ability to exercise power.**
>
> **It is far more important to acknowledge leaders when they display some of the desired behavior than it is to correct them because they have not effected all of it.**
>
> **Catching leaders in the act of "doing the right thing" helps them form a permanent memory of what the desired behavior looks and feels like.**
>
> **Acknowledging small, positive changes builds confidence about change itself and the rewards change brings.**

Disconfirmation is needed when appropriate, but we must make sure that we are even more quick to notice and acknowledge improvements.

COPING WITH RECURRING BEHAVIOR

When there are too few examples of a leader doing the right thing and too many of continuing the offending behavior, both disconfirmation and coping mechanisms are needed.

We'll find ourselves better prepared to give disconfirming feedback if we get the leader's agreement on our role:

> **"Would it help if I mention it if I observe you doing this again?"**

If leaders agree intellectually that change is important, but for whatever reason they are not actually making that change, they should be open to the group developing coping mechanisms to minimize the effect of their behavior. Coping mechanisms combine ways of empowering the group to behave functionally with consequences that disconfirm the leader's disruptive behavior. Examples include the following:

> **If the leader chronically comes to work at 10:00 a.m., she will not require staff who start at 8:00 a.m. to do support work in the evenings.**

> **If the leader bottlenecks communications that require her signature, staff will be empowered to take them off her desk after three days and sign for her.**

> **If the leader screams and abuses staff, they will get up and leave until she regains self-control.**

> **If the leader dominates meetings, she will put five dollars in a kitty for each statement that cuts off group input, as will anyone in the group who cuts off others.**

Agreed-on consequences remove the feedback process from the verbal level and place it on the action level. This is important, as a follower may be reluctant to appear to be the nag by continuously harping on the recurring behavior.

Recognizing that there are consequences to behavior is a key element in the transformation process. Self-initiated consequences provide leaders with symbols of potentially harsher public consequences should their behavior remain unchanged. And agreed-on coping mechanisms give followers a way of taking care of their needs and the needs of the organization while the leader works to improve.

REALISTIC EXPECTATIONS

The roots of the attitudes and behaviors we seek to transform may be planted in body memories formed long before we learned to ride a bicycle, and they may last just as long as that remarkable piece of programming.

When we grow up speaking one language and learn another later in life, we will retain the accent of the first. Our mouth and tongue have learned to form certain shapes and continue to do so. We can reduce the accent, but not eliminate it. So it is with the core behaviors of our personality. It will help us remain supportive if we bear in mind a few things about transformation efforts:

> **Don't expect perfect responses; leaders are no more perfect than we are.**
>
> **Expect to see more balance between strengths and weaknesses, not a total transformation of character.**
>
> **Look for a shift in emphasis between competing values—perhaps more concern for the people and process and less for the outcome regardless of human costs.**
>
> **Expect more consciousness of certain actions and the effects the actions have, not the immediate cessation of those actions.**
>
> **Recognize that when individuals become aware of doing something "wrong," it is a precursor to their being able to check themselves and do it differently.**
>
> **Anticipate regression under pressure; recognize it as a natural part of the learning cycle and an opportunity for further growth.**

We can acknowledge our disappointment or anger when we see old behaviors still at work, but not let those feelings derail our support for the process. The courageous follower participates in transformation within the larger context of the group's mission and doesn't fixate on the failure to transform every detail and action. We are aiming for better balance and the ability to achieve the organization's purpose. These are realistic and important expectations.

PERSISTENCE

In transformation, as in virtually every human activity, persistence is often the difference between success and failure. If we do not persist, we "give up," and those who give up are no longer assuming responsibility for the situation. To a greater or lesser degree, they become alienated.

Alienation is not conducive to the growth of the follower, the leader, or the organization. An organization being hurt by a leader's dysfunctional behavior is further hurt by losing the committed energy of followers. The common purpose severely suffers.

There are many reasons that change may not be happening as quickly as we would like:

> The timing may be wrong.

> Distractions in the environment may overwhelm the effort.

> The intervention may be inadequate; we may need to seek a second opinion, as we would in a deteriorating medical situation.

> The consequences may still be too remote to provide motivation.

> The effort may be undermined by actions from a more senior level or another influence.

> Our own transformation may not be far enough along to serve as a catalyst for the leader's transformation.

For the leader and follower, as for any people in a relationship, commitment and stick-to-it-iveness are needed to overcome adversity and work out interpersonal difficulties.

When leaders try to improve an organization's awareness and behavior, they find many ways of sending their message throughout the organization. Customer service campaigns, for example, run for years with training, speeches, newsletters, posters, videos, focus groups, reengineering processes, incentive programs, award ceremonies, and so on. When followers try to raise leaders' awareness and influence their choices, they may also need to find many ways of getting the message across.

Transformation requires patience and determination, creativity and determination, determination and more determination.

A courageous follower's art is to persist without letting the effort deteriorate into a power struggle. The follower's need to make an impact cannot drive the process. The drivers must continue to be the common purpose and the welfare of the leader, the organization, and those the organization serves.

If we get haughty, if we become arrogant about the leader, we have become "hooked." Something in our own psyche, something of our own issues with power has been triggered. We can't lead the leader in areas we have not ourselves addressed. We would do better to work on these for a while rather than unproductively butt egos with the leader.

We must remember that more change may be happening under the surface than is apparent from the leader's visible behavior. The struggle is like hatching an egg—a lot of work is done inside the shell where others can't see it before the first cracks, let alone a hole large enough to step through, appear. Just when we think we cannot reach this person, that she is not capable of change, she may make her breakthrough—darkness before the dawn. Just when we think we cannot make this relationship work, *we* may have our own breakthrough that unlocks it.

VALIDATION

When transformation occurs, it should be acknowledged. We all believe we are good people. When that belief has been challenged and we have walked the difficult road of attempting to match reality with our beliefs, we deserve to hear about that as clearly as we heard about our flaws. This does not mean validating transformation at the first sign of improvement, because premature validation can demotivate the leader. It does mean validating sustained change:

> "I'd like you to know how consistently I see you doing _____."

> "I want you to know I no longer experience _____ in our relationship and what a difference that has made."

"In the last few months, I've felt better than ever about how we work together."

"I've heard a lot of admiration from the field about how you _____."

"In my estimation, the results we are now achieving are due in no small part to the change you've made in _____."

"My hat's off to you. It took a lot of courage to do what you did."

We may achieve many victories in our lives, but genuine transformation is often the hardest and most precious. When we are close to a leader who has been transformed, we should bear witness to that transformation, both to the leader and to the world. Validation helps strengthen the fibers of new patterns so they wear well through the fraying challenges that lie ahead.

6

THE COURAGE TO
TAKE MORAL ACTION

MOST ACTIVITIES WE ENGAGE IN fall well within the boundaries of what we consider to be morally right. But sometimes we perceive that boundary being approached or crossed. These ethical junctures require us to examine and clarify our own values and wrestle with the tension between what we feel is right and what opportunities exist for personal gain or loss. We find ourselves face to face with our wonderful and burdensome capacity for free will. The choices we make will define or redefine our character and perhaps our reputation.

In organizational life, this activity is made more complex. Not only do we need to wrestle with these questions in terms of our own choices and behaviors, but we sometimes encounter situations in which we need to take a moral position in relation to the choices and behaviors of our colleagues and, in particular, our leaders. If we have questioned and challenged behavior that crosses or threatens to cross a moral boundary, and that behavior persists, we will be faced with the need to make additional choices.

For example, terrific pressure may exist in an organization to make a key measurement of organizational performance look good by using short-sighted, questionable, or deceptive means. This pressure is symptomatic of deeper organizational dynamics that may or may not be within the capability of a follower to control or influence. Nevertheless, the follower is faced with the choice of whether to go along with the prevailing culture or to take a stand that may generate unpleasant and difficult personal consequences. As difficult as taking a stand may be, failure to do so has had disastrous consequences to organizations, their leaders, and the followers who acquiesced to pressure when the actions they took crossed ethical and legal lines. It is in these situations where the courage to take moral action becomes necessary.

What is a moral stand? There are many levels of action or refusal to act, each of which represents a moral stand. Sometimes it is sufficient to choose and act on one level. At other times, a series of choices that build on each other is necessary. One may take a morally motivated action that has the least potential for personal repercussions knowing that if this action proves insufficient, another level of action will be required. The gamut of moral stances may run from refusing to participate in a morally dubious conversation or activity, to refusing to remain in the group if it proceeds with the activity, to publicly opposing the activity. In addition, a variety of intermediate steps surround each of these levels.

Because a courageous follower operates from a sense of loyalty to the common purpose that the organization serves, morally motivated behavior must also factor in the impact of any action, or refusal to act, on the organization itself. One might choose a course of action that succeeds in stopping the morally objectionable behavior but seriously weakens or even destroys a worthwhile organization in the process. Has one behaved morally? This is an important and quite different reason to take incremental steps when confronting morally objectionable behavior if there is a reasonable chance that those steps can lead to the correction of the offending behavior.

 Moral action is taken with the intention of bringing the actions of the leadership and organization into line with fundamental values that govern decent organizational behavior while preserving the capacity of the organization to fulfill its purpose.

Failing this, the minimal fallback position of moral action is to refrain from participating in the immoral or morally dubious behavior oneself.

Assuming that a follower has already exercised the courage to challenge and to participate in transformation, the actions to contemplate under the heading "The Courage to Take Moral Action" revolve around several points. These include the decision of whether to appeal to higher levels of authority within the organization, whether to stay in or leave an organization, how to frame conversations and actions around these decision-making processes, and how to conduct oneself in the face of different potential outcomes.

The stakes can be very high for an individual faced with these moral choices since they often involve the risk of leaving or being forced by the organization to leave under very strained circumstances. In the United

States, in recent memory, we have twice seen examples of the attorney general, the highest-ranking law enforcement officer in the government, resign or be prepared to resign in the face of misuse of power by the president of the United States whom they served. Democracies owe their gratitude to public servants who take moral stands to protect the rule of law.

Although we rarely find ourselves at critical crossroads such as these, when we do, it is vital we make morally grounded decisions. I know personally how difficult this can be. In my mid-thirties, I found that I had devoted a significant portion of my adult life to an organization and its leader that were increasingly at odds with my values and vision. Initially, I couldn't acknowledge my discomfort with the leader's actions. I manifested the conflict I felt through stress-induced illness. Only when I became persona non grata for participating in an internal reform effort did I confront the fact that it was truly time to separate.

But for some of my contemporaries in the organization, leaving wasn't enough. They felt it important to publicly oppose the organization's practices. Still others, who were also uncomfortable with the practices, felt duty bound to stay with the organization and try to be change agents from within. This is a personal decision. There is not necessarily a moral imperative to choose one course or the other. But it is important that we make the decision consciously.

Healthy followership is a conscious act of free will. When we no longer believe that what we are doing is the best thing or the right thing, we must review our options and their respective consequences. Otherwise, we are in danger of becoming automatons with a dulled sense of responsibility for our actions, who serve neither ourselves, the leader, the common purpose nor society well.

LEAVING

Although moral action does not always require leaving a group or organization, it always implies the potential of leaving if the offending situation is not corrected or, indeed, if we ourselves have offended the core values of the group. Therefore, we must examine the dynamics of contemplating leaving a group, whether as a natural act of growth or as the outcome of taking a moral stand.

Merging and separating are two of the most basic acts of life. At different stages of our lives, we form or leave relationships. From birth to death this is a profound act. In the middle there may be loves found and lost, loyalties given and withdrawn, positions occupied and abandoned.

Giving part of ourselves to another is a fundamental act of family, groups, and society. The ability to reclaim that part of ourselves is equally fundamental. Faced with the death of a beloved spouse, we need to find a way to again live without the other. Faced with an abusive spouse, we need to find a way to extricate ourselves from the damaging relationship and make our own way in the world. When we outgrow a group, or when it stagnates and we cannot rejuvenate it, or when it betrays our loyalty, we need to move on to other groups that can fill our needs and utilize our contributions.

Each of these acts requires courage. For better or worse, the known is predictable; the unknown is not. Can we succeed, or even survive, when we leave the familiar situation? We don't know until we try. There are many valid reasons for a courageous follower to separate from a leader, ranging from the benign to the lifethreatening.

GROWTH

The most benign, natural reason to move on is growth. Leaders mentor us; we learn and grow. At some point we are ready to move from under their shadow. We are ready to seek other mentors, to test what we have learned, to serve in ways we have discovered we were meant to serve, or to explore what those ways might be.

We may admire or even love the leader. But it is time to go. It is time to better define ourselves independently, even if doing so proves to be preparation for returning to serve the leader and our common purpose in new ways.

As stewards of the purpose, we make detailed preparations to transfer responsibilities so that service to the leader and organization continues uninterrupted. We leave without a sudden rupture.

GROUP OPTIMIZATION

Group optimization is the reverse side of the coin of leaving for our personal growth; it means the leader and organization may need to grow. Sometimes a leader needs fresh input. The loyalty and experience of long-serving followers may be outweighed by a stasis of new ideas. A calcification of methods serves the common purpose poorly.

A time may come when we sense the organization's need for new blood. Or it is pointed out to us by others. A courageous follower acknowledges when this is true, recognizing that the right infusion can rejuvenate the leader and organization. The challenge is to accept this passage as a natural flow of life, not as a personal failing; to take advantage of the opportunity to examine our own needs and explore new ways to better meet these.

When members of a high-performance team separate for reasons of personal growth or group optimization, and then join or form other organizations, the original group doesn't die so much as it transforms into a living network. If the relationships have been kept healthy and the separation is done well, a new kind of power emerges from the bonds between people who are connected through their fields and across disciplines.

EXHAUSTION

If we become exhausted, we lose our ability to serve the common purpose. If we have not managed ourselves well or are being used up by a leader, we may need to separate in order to reclaim and rejuvenate ourselves.

The nurturing a follower receives from a leader does not have to be equal to that which a follower gives a leader, but it must be present and meaningful. If it is not and we are unsuccessful at changing this dynamic, the self-responsible act may be to leave.

PRINCIPLED ACTION

Courageous followership is principled followership. If we have failed to serve the common purpose in some important way, we must be willing to resign the position given us in trust. If a leader is failing to serve the common purpose in some important way and will not recognize or change this shortcoming, courageous followers may need to tender their resignation as the only principled option available.

The need to leave, especially as a principled act, is not difficult to grasp intellectually or morally, but it can nevertheless appear daunting and take time to accept. We need to prepare ourselves for the eventuality.

DIFFICULTY OF SEPARATION

In a relationship between dynamic leaders and committed followers who share a common purpose, withdrawing support from a leader is a wrenching act. It is closer to the experience of divorce than it is to leaving one job for another. As in a divorce, it can take months to begin recovering from the experience and years to fully recover.

The leader won the loyalty of followers because of a shared commitment to a common purpose and the many attractive attributes the leader brought to the pursuit of that purpose. Whether or not these attributes have been obscured by less attractive ones, the prospect of leaving can stir up conflicted feelings in the follower.

There are many scenarios in which separation is difficult. If a leader and organization are failing, the most painful loss may be that of our dreams, of the expectations we had for the organization, its cause, and our own future. We may need to mourn these losses in order to fully separate.

Fearing the loss of reflected power from the leader also causes reluctance to separate. We come to believe that our ability to live a meaningful life and maintain a sense of control over our destiny are dependent on the leader's fortune. We may need to rediscover our internal compass and our own power. Though some people will stop replying to our messages and cease being supportive when we lose our reflected power, we'll soon discover the genuine relationships in our lives.

Sometimes we become overly specialized, having served a particular organization and leader for many years. We wonder how we will survive; who would want us if we leave? Sometimes we just lose the habit of how to live outside the organization. Followers working in intense environments that demand round-the-clock activity, such as senior political offices, advocacy groups, or start-up companies in highly competitive industries, are particularly prone to sacrificing time with their families and communities. They need to regain familiarity with living a balanced life.

Separation difficulty is ultimately a crisis of identity. We are no longer sure of who we are, independent of the organization. The organization forms an important part of our identity in an age when other institutions that traditionally have given people a sense of belonging have weakened. This is seen in its extreme form in cults, whose members cease belonging to any other unit in society and derive their identity nearly completely from cult membership. But the phenomenon is a widespread occurrence in less intense forms: witness recent retirees or people whose jobs have been eliminated. Drawing our identity from involvement in an organization raises the emotional stakes of leaving.

Followers struggling with separation might ask themselves these questions:

"Who am I on my own?"

"What do I believe?"

"What do I want?"

"Is the organization's purpose still my purpose?"

"Are there other ways to pursue this purpose?"

"What do I really need to survive?"

"What are my skills?"

"What else could I do with these skills?"

"What gives me satisfaction?"

"What would I be willing to take risks for?"

"Who are my real friends?"

"What do I owe the leader and the organization?"

"What do they owe me?"

"How can we discharge these obligations to each other?"

Our identity is never really lost, just obscured. We are wise to maintain relationships and interests outside the organization, for their own sake as well as for their importance in retaining our independent identity. This will make leaving the leader and organization considerably easier when the time comes to do so.

FINANCIAL CONTINGENCIES

Most followers are not independently wealthy. The financial factors involved in leaving are often as weighty as the emotional factors. If leaving is a considered decision made mutually with the leader, we usually have little financial problem in making the transition. But we will also examine a range of circumstances in which the separation may be sudden. If our principles require us to resign or to take a confrontational stand that may lead to dismissal, financial factors come into play, sometimes decisively.

If we don't have financial contingency plans in place, our courage may be offset by our responsibilities. Many of us are contributing to the support of a family. Some are the sole support. Few of us can weather prolonged unemployment or a dramatic pay cut without seriously affecting our standard of living. Yet staying in a position for financial reasons, when doing so no longer serves us or the common purpose, can psychologically and spiritually exact as great a toll as unemployment does.

Particularly if the environment has become abusive, we can experience a terrible internal values conflict: On the one hand, intellectual honesty, moral integrity, and self-esteem cry out for us to speak the truth as we see it. On the other hand, responsibility for our family, investment in our career, and yearning for security act as restraining forces against our speaking candidly. It is healthy for followers to develop financial contingency plans so that fear of losing our position never prevents us from speaking the truth about ourselves or our leaders. Paradoxically, such plans are also healthy for leaders because their existence improves the prospects of leaders receiving honest feedback.

Financial contingency plans might include the following:

> Money in the bank that enables us to "walk away" and still meet our financial obligations until we can reestablish ourselves

> Agreement with a spouse or partner to support each other if one of us must leave our employment for reasons of conscience, until we can find or develop another opportunity

> Establishing an ample line of credit while we are in a strong position to do so

> Continuing to live within our former means when we are elevated to a higher position, so that we can afford to lose that position

> Staying visible in our field, to improve our chances for a successful lateral move if we leave the organization

> Maintaining a sideline business, hobby, or other marketable skills that we can further develop if we must leave our field

> Negotiating a contract that clearly spells out terms of severance we can live with.

Every generation observes the idealism and risk taking of youth replaced by the pragmatic conservatism of age. As we age, we usually have more to lose. Our risk taking is replaced by another type of courage—the courage to be responsible for others. If we can put financial contingency plans in place, we are in a stronger position to remain pragmatic without sacrificing our ideals.

OFFERING TO RESIGN

Whereas separation from an organization may be a long, well-considered process, resignation based on principles is often abrupt. We can resign because of our own breach of trust or in protest of the leader's. We'll examine the former situation first.

From the day courageous followers assume a position of trust close to a prominent leader, they must be prepared to resign if they break that trust. Leaders and their teams are trusted to vigorously pursue the common purpose within the framework of community and organizational values. Even the appearance of having broken that trust may require resignation. It is best to mentally prepare for this eventuality from the start. When circumstances demanding resignation occur, we usually have little time and scant mental and emotional resources to think things through.

The need to offer our resignation in the face of a breach of trust develops out of a sense of why we are there and whom we serve. Resigning can be a statement of commitment to the common purpose and an act of confirming community values. It is not egoless, but ego respecting—we have too much respect for ourselves, the leader, and the organization to be found wriggling out of our moral obligations.

Under these circumstances, a resignation needs to be tendered quickly to make an effective moral statement. If it is offered belatedly, it appears to be what it is—bowing to pressure—rather than an honorable recognition of the real or perceived breach of trust. An effective resignation can itself be a redemptive act. At this stage, considerations about our own welfare and what we will do next are inappropriate. Of course, these anxieties are present, but they are outside the imperative of our decision.

At the same time, a resignation is not offered lightly. It is not an appropriate response to every mistake. We cannot demand perfection of ourselves any more than we can demand it of our leaders. Organizations and individuals pursue their purpose and meet their objectives by doing and failing and learning and doing. Nor does a courageous follower resign to avoid responsibility for cleaning up a mess. It may take more courage to stay on the scene and spend years unraveling the consequences of our actions than it does to leave.

Sometimes, offering to resign is protective of the leader, showing respect for his values and helping distance him from a debacle he did not cause, from actions he did not sanction. A resignation can be a courageous act that clarifies accountability. But taking the fall for a leader who caused or significantly contributed to the debacle obscures accountability and may not serve the common purpose well.

Early in their relationship with a leader, courageous followers should establish criteria for resignation:

> "Under what circumstances must I resign? What types of activities would violate the core values of this organization and its community?"

> "Under what circumstances should I consider resigning? What activities would appear to violate the organization's values, even if they represent poor judgment rather than betrayal of trust?"

> "Under what circumstances should I hold my ground? When would it serve the organization to do so, even if it hurts me or the leadership?"

Thinking through these questions can clarify values and formulate guidelines for future actions. This clarity may prevent real or perceived violations of trust from occurring.

If it is appropriate to offer to resign, the courageous follower approaches the leader with speed and deliberation. If the leader concurs with the follower's decision to resign, they decide together how to announce and implement the decision. The resignation becomes a final team effort that confirms the organization's values, minimizes disruption to the organization's pursuit of its purpose, and respects the overall contributions of the follower.

QUERY AND APPEAL

Once we have prepared ourselves for the possibility of leaving the organization, we can examine other strategies available to us that may or may not lead to the necessity to do so.

Presumably we have already had conversations in which we questioned the order and those conversations did not result in it being amended or withdrawn. We can now query the order in writing to our direct supervisor from whom it was received. Querying an order in writing serves several functions:

> It gives us an opportunity to restate the order as we understood it and verify that it is what was meant by the supervisor who issued it.

> It gives the individual issuing the order a chance to reflect on it further as she considers your response.

> It begins a document trail that will put everyone on alert that this will be a matter of record, so they should be sure it is a legal order and one that they are prepared to defend to others.

If the issuer of the order knows there is some question as to the ethics or good judgment behind it, this simple act often is enough to cause a reevaluation and amendment or withdrawal of the order.

If we still find ourselves at an impasse with our direct supervisor and morally uncomfortable with the order or policy, we have the option of querying or appealing it to a higher level of authority. When this option is available, it is often the correct moral action to take, but doing so is fraught with sensitivities.

The first sensitivity is our relationship with our direct superior who is issuing the order. If we have a good relationship with this individual, we will, of course, raise our concern with him. If he maintains his position despite our clear expressions of concern, we are faced with the prospect of going above him and creating complications for this individual whom we otherwise respect. Conversely, if we already have a strained relationship with our superior, it may be tempting to avoid him altogether and go directly to the next level of authority, which will further strain the relationship.

In these cases, the guiding principle is to tend to our relationship as best we can while still doing what we believe is right. Under normal circumstances, this involves informing our superior of our intentions:

> "You and I seem to have a fundamental disagreement on this matter. I would like us to consult with _____ [next level of authority] before we implement this action."

> "I know that you have said that _____ [next level of authority] has sanctioned this activity, but I am still uncomfortable with it and need to speak directly with her before proceeding. Would you like to sit in on the meeting so we each can present our concerns?"

Sometimes we feel too personally threatened to be this open with our direct superior regarding our intentions. We may be tempted not to give prior notice before going to a higher level. Courageous followership requires challenging ourselves as to whether this is truly necessary. Might our concerns be exaggerated? What will be the consequences to our group dynamics when our direct superior learns of our action, which will probably happen?

The second sensitivity in deciding whether to query or appeal an order or policy to a higher level is the likely reaction at that level. These actions carry two different levels of risk.

Querying an order or policy is a request for clarification before proceeding to enact it. Its intention is to prevent inadvertently making serious mistakes because of faulty information or communication. Depending on whether the higher level of authority is the originator or not, a query seeks to have answered certain questions:

> Is the order or policy being relayed as intended?

> Has the higher level of authority been given full information about the context in which the order or policy will be executed?

> Has the higher level of authority fully considered the potential consequences of implementing the order or policy as it stands?

> Have the highest levels of authority who will be held accountable for the action been thoroughly briefed on these factors?

> Can those issuing the orders provide further information that will help those who are expected to implement the actions understand the reasoning behind them?

An *appeal*, by contrast, is an explicit request to cancel, alter, or delay implementation of an order or policy. It may follow a query that has not resulted in concerns being satisfactorily addressed, or it may be made without first requesting further clarification.

> "Respectfully, I request this order be rescinded for the following reasons: _____ ."
>
> "Based on the reasons I have stated, I am requesting that you make the following amendments to the policy before it is broadly issued: _____ ."
>
> "I have fully discussed my objections to this proposed directive with _____ [direct superior], and she is still intent on issuing it. Because of the potential damage to our mission, and despite my generally high regard for _____ , I am taking the unusual step of asking you to intervene and suspend the directive until you have had a chance to fully study the issue."

As followers, we must appreciate that the higher level of authority to whom we are making the appeal also has a relationship with our direct superior. She must do what she can to protect the common purpose and values of the organization and also be sensitive to the morale and development of her direct report, who may have made an error in judgment.

We may find the actions that result from our appeal mitigate the most troubling aspects of the order or policy without fully addressing our concerns. As courageous followers, we must once again evaluate what will serve the common purpose best. If we can now morally live with the imperfect outcome of this process, that may be the best way to serve the common purpose.

For most of us, and in most of the situations in which we will ever find ourselves, the relatively simple acts of querying or appealing orders will be sufficient to resolve situations in which we are morally uncomfortable. In rare situations, the situation goes beyond this and we are more severely tested. If we still cannot or should not live with the order or policy, even after it has been modified in response to our concerns or, more problematically, if we find that the higher levels of authority fully agree with the original order or policy that disturbs us, we will need to contemplate tak-ing the next level of moral action.

THE DUTY TO DISOBEY

There are times when we cannot convince leaders to change their policies or actions, and we gracefully line up with the team and support the poli-cies. There are other times when the policies or actions are morally unac-ceptable to us. In this case, a courageous follower must consider refusing to participate in their implementation.

The right to refuse and the duty to refuse implementing a policy or order are almost indistinguishable; they should be exercised under nearly identi-cal circumstances. If we receive a policy or order that we feel is destructive to fundamental values and the common purpose, our right and duty to refuse to implement the policy or order are activated. We have the duty to disobey even if the whole group obeys. This requires profound courage because the pressure to conform is enormous. Not only do we need the courage to voice our decision to disobey, but we must also find additional courage to sus-tain our decision when we are cajoled or threatened into changing it.

No fast rules can be devised to guide our decision to disobey; each act is one of principle taken within the context of a specific and unique situation. There are times when values conflict. For example, values formed in differ-ent cultures may be inherently polarized. Compassion, intelligence, self-esteem, and perhaps even a little higher guidance are needed to determine when refusing to comply is the correct and necessary action. What kinds of circumstances might warrant refusing to implement a policy or order?

Human life or health are being unnecessarily risked.

Common decency is being violated.

The rule of law is being sacrificed to expediency.

The organization's purpose is being undermined.

The organization's stakeholders are being denied basic service.

A clique or special interest is being served at the expense of the common good.

It is even more important to reject a policy or order when others' rights and welfare are jeopardized rather than our own. This is how the fabric of the social order is kept whole. While disobedience on behalf of another may be more clearly defensible, the integrity required is greater because there is so little to be gained for ourselves, so much to be lost.

How we convey our refusal to disobey is contextual. In a situation in which we are given a verbal order that we must act or not act on immediately, such as in a police or military action, the stand will most likely be oral or real-time text messaging. If we have the presence of mind to state clearly why we will not obey, this can be germane in future disciplinary reviews of the decision, especially if witnesses were present:

> "Sir, you need to rescind that order, or _____ [state severe operational consequences that will result]."

> "I request you withdraw that order because _____ [state immediate threat to life, health, etc.]."

> "I cannot comply with that order as it violates _____ [code, law, regulation]."

In a situation that does not have instant life-and-death level of consequences, our approach can be different. Requesting a private meeting or committing our concerns in thoughtfully worded writing will, for reasons we have already examined, generally be more effective.

When we take a courageous stance by refusing to implement instructions, we sincerely believe our actions are right and necessary. It may turn out, however, that our decision to disobey was wrong and carried serious consequences for the group. Fear of error should make us appropriately cautious but not paralyze us. We have to be prepared to shoulder the responsibility for our mistakes, too.

If an act of disobedience comes under formal review, it is hoped that those who sit in judgment will examine the motives that drove the act. If the act sprang from fundamental values of decency and concern for the common purpose, it is hoped they will weigh that against the value of compliance to authority and judge accordingly.

THREATENING TO RESIGN

If we express our intention to disobey a morally offensive order, or if we disobey one and are overridden, we must be as prepared to resign in protest as we are prepared to resign should our own breach of trust warrant it. The implicit power to withdraw support is one of the powers that permits a follower to influence events. It is always present and is usually unstated. In organizations where followers have served leaders for a protracted time, the follower's continued loyalty may be taken for granted. If a leader does not treat seriously the need for change, a follower may need to exercise that power to withdraw support through an explicit warning.

Not only must we tell leaders *how* we feel, but we must tell them how *intensely* we feel about issues that concern us. In collections of people that are not committed to the group, individuals will just leave if they are discontented. They do not engage in uncomfortable, energy-demanding confrontation. In a committed group, members will speak up clearly and forcefully before exercising the option to leave.

The warning of impending resignation, if not used lightly, is one of the legitimate ways to voice the depth of our concern. If we are viewed as a loyal follower, the fact that we would consider leaving over the issue strengthens the impact of what we are saying.

> "I must advise you this is a decision I cannot live with. I believe it places our people at unnecessary and unacceptable risk."

> "I need to be clear about this. I will not be able to go along with that approach as I believe it violates our basic principles."

> "If you insist on issuing that order, I will need to step aside as I cannot implement it in good conscience."

> "If we cannot agree to modify our position, regretfully I will need to resign as I cannot be party to it."

When fundamental values conflict, when core policy differences are not treated seriously, or when transformation efforts deteriorate to lip service, threatening to withdraw support is an important moral tool. If we communicate that the potential consequences of these conditions include our resignation, we may elevate an issue so it is viewed with sufficient gravity for change to occur. And if we don't succeed, the situation has been unmistakably clarified and can inform our decision to stay or leave.

THE DILEMMA OF THE "UNREASONABLE" LEADER

The "unreasonable" man or woman is sometimes said to be the primary agent of change in a culture. Reasonable people adapt to their surroundings; "unreasonable" individuals change those surroundings to better suit their needs. The strength of an unreasonable leader is the ability to think outside the current paradigm and envision entirely new possibilities. This is the leader who comes in and turns a place on its ear. Suddenly everything feels different. Expectations are astronomically higher. Stability is not valued. Change is initiated everywhere. Old assumptions are flushed into the open and challenged. The pace is significantly accelerated. Relationships are altered. The universe is no longer as we knew it.

"Unreasonable" leaders can make even courageous followers uncomfortable with the scope and rate of change. We may resist such leaders and be fearful of the consequences of their actions. Yet these may be the very actions that the organization needs to survive or to create breakthroughs. In our inability to see beyond our paradigm, to appreciate the leader's prescience, to cope with the discomfort created, we may be tempted to withdraw our support though the leader fully deserves it.

How can we differentiate between our inertia and fears and our legitimate concerns for the organization in the hands of an iconoclastic leader? Once again, values and purpose must be our guiding lights:

> **Are the core values of the community and organization being respected?** (Not the norms, but the core values.)
>
> **Are peripheral values that do not forward the common purpose being challenged?** In a social service agency, for example, going easy on staff and not pushing them may have become a value that lowered the quantity and quality of badly needed services.
>
> **Are the twin tests of honesty and decency being met?** They are important barometers of the respect being shown for core values;

if the leader is communicating honestly and people are treated decently, even when they have to be moved aside to get the job done, power is being used, not abused.

Is the flurry of actions being taken geared to achieve the common purpose and not some other agenda of the leader's?

Are the risks being taken justified? The "unreasonable" leader may take high risks, as leaders sometimes must, but those high risks should outweigh the risks of inaction or "safe" action.

Are the processes of group input respected while being accelerated, so that the organization becomes a stronger team, more capable of achieving its purpose over time?

If values are being respected and the purpose is being served, we can get aboard the leader's express. If they are not, his actions must be challenged. Brilliance and dynamism without strong, decent values are untrustworthy vehicles for power, regardless of their expediency.

VALUES REVIEW

The actions of a leader who is abusing power can be so at odds with his proclaimed values that cognitive dissonance prevents us from fully registering the discrepancies. But we do experience discomfort at the perimeters of our awareness and must try to pay attention to it.

Whether we become aware of the values conflict gradually or because of some isolated episode that assaults our sense of decency, this awareness must trigger a hard review of the leader's actual values. To conduct a values review, we can do the following:

Compile a list of what we hold to be basic values of human decency.

Compile a list of which of these the leader purports to share.

Compile a list of recent actions taken by the leader.

Review which actions support our sense of basic human values and which conflict with them.

After completing the values review, we must make a decision:

> If the leader's actions largely support our values and do not egregiously violate any of them, we should continue our support.

> If the leader's actions largely conflict with our values or egregiously violate core values, we must be prepared to withdraw our support.

The critical differentiation in this process is between statements and actions. Leaders who violate values attempt to obfuscate the record with explanations. As long as we believe a leader is serving the common purpose, we would like to believe those explanations. We are prone to deny abusive acts. We may even become apologists for them. A hard look at actions clarifies the situation.

FOLLOWER SELF-EXAMINATION

When courageous followers believe that neither the organization's values nor its purpose is being served well by the leader, and they are considering withdrawing support, they should also examine themselves before acting.

In many organizational cultures, colleagues sympathize with us if we gripe to them about the leader. Friends and family do, too. We can mistake this as strong support for the righteousness of our views. To ensure that our actions will benefit the organization and those it serves, we must seek good counsel just as we encourage our leaders to do. To help us discern right-motivated action, we may take the following precautions:

> We can ask for guidance from our peers, for feedback on how they perceive our reactions to the leader.

> We should choose these peers for their diversity and honesty, not just for their history of supporting us.

> We should frame our concerns in a nonincendiary way, so that the healthy act of examination isn't misconstrued as incitement and held against us if we decide we are not justified in withdrawing support.

We should not ask for our peers' views in order to manipulate them into our position or reduce our own responsibility for our decision.

We should seek as much objectivity as we can get, not to replace our inevitable subjectivity but to test it.

We must be as open to challenge as we wish our leader to be; we must try to behave in the way that we are concerned he does not.

If peers advise against withdrawing support because they feel we are off the mark, involved in our own issues with authority, power grabbing, or failing to see the larger picture, their advice must be taken seriously. If they caution not to withdraw support because of the potential personal consequences, courageous followers may elect to ignore this advice and put values and purpose first.

THE DECISION TO WITHDRAW SUPPORT

The bottom line of followership is that we are responsible for our decision to continue or not to continue following a leader. Even *in extremis*, we have the choice of supporting an anathema to our values or not. This is the Nuremberg trials principle. The fact that we are following orders absolves us from nothing. Of course, this choice is made in the context of our full values structures. Competing values, such as love for and responsibility to our family, may make the choice difficult, even excruciating, but we always have choices and are responsible for the ones we make.

If we have honestly examined ourselves and energetically worked to help a leader transform, yet we still find a significant gap between a leader's actions and our core values, we have to give very serious consideration to withdrawing our support. Commitment is central to a relationship, but it does not necessarily bind us if the relationship is stagnant or destructive despite our energetic efforts to improve it.

When the relationship principles examined in this guide fail to help a leader maintain a balanced use of power, the difficulty may stem from psychological roots that are beyond the reach of a follower's influence. It is critical that we recognize when our ability to influence a situation has been exceeded, when withdrawal is the appropriate course.

The duty to withdraw support increases in proportion to the egregiousness of the violation of values and our proximity to the leader. Our responsibility as close followers is great because often only the inner circle sees the leader's true values at an early stage; others may still see only the public persona. We can protect a values-deficient leader and allow him to amass power, or we can strip away the camouflage we are providing.

When courageous followers withdraw support from a leader, it will help to bear in mind the following:

> If we are among the first in a group to withdraw support, we will need the conviction of our values, confidence in our powers of observation, and the courage to maintain our isolated position.

> When we separate from a leader, we must also question whether the common purpose we shared with the leader is valid.

> If the purpose is valid, we must examine our commitment to it independent of our relationship with the leader and identify other ways, consistent with our commitment, of pursuing that purpose.

> We will add to the emotional and material cost of separation if we continue supporting a cause out of unexamined habit or if we abandon a cause, organization, or project that is close to our heart.

> If we leave and later events prove we were wrong about the leader, we should use the experience to learn more about our relationships with leaders, but we should never berate ourselves for having had the courage to act on our convictions.

When we withdraw support, we may need to come to terms with many things, including why we gave our support for as long as we did, what actions we took in the name of the cause or activity, and any sense of loss and regret. None of this is easy, but it is far more preferable to compounding the situation by lacking the courage to withdraw from it.

THE RESPONSIBILITY TO
BLOW THE WHISTLE

The decision to withdraw support from a leader does not automatically require disavowing that leader. Followers may simply decide there are more important purposes and more values-centered leaders to support or that they are ready to test their own leadership abilities. We can withdraw amicably without detailing our reasons. This is the most common way of leaving. Résumés and references, if not relationships, mostly stay intact.

However, there are circumstances when followers have further obligations. When a leader's actions seriously endanger the organization or community, silent withdrawal is inappropriate. We need to draw public scrutiny to those actions. When respect for human life, the welfare of children, or the rule of law and other basic moral values are violated, a line is crossed. Public exposure is a primary tool for disempowering leaders who abuse their power or who permit others in the organization to do so.

Somewhere at this juncture it can be said that an individual crosses a line from courageous follower to whistleblower. Not all whistleblowers are courageous followers. Some are angry individuals who, based on their own histories, do not trust authority and are seeking retribution for perceived wrongs Others may be timid. They have not really given their leadership a fair opportunity to correct the wrongdoing that they have discovered. Public disclosure can be premature, irrevocably damage their relationships, and hurt their organization's ability to perform its mission.

Conversely, not all courageous followers are whistleblowers, if the term is used to mean going around the leader or even outside the organization to remedy a wrong. Often, courageous followers work with their leaders to remedy situations they have discovered. The most successful have no need to become whistleblowers. Of course, whether they feel the need to cross over the line and become a whistleblower depends on the response of their leaders to their efforts to remedy organizational wrongdoing.

If leaders at the various levels of the organization to which we have access fail to respond when serious transgressions are brought to their attention, or seem to stall and endlessly delay action, we must consider going around them for intervention. Most large organizations have a variety of internal corrective channels that can be approached for recourse, including boards of directors. If these, too, are unresponsive, we should once more examine our own position, our data, and our presentation very thoroughly. If after further thorough self examination we are still disturbed by what we witness, we must honor this discomfort and pay attention to the cognitive dissonance between what we want to believe of our leaders and what we are observing. As loyal followers, we must first disavow ourselves of the idea that things will improve if the evidence points overwhelmingly to the contrary. There comes a point when we cannot believe words. We can only believe actions.

When our leaders' actions violate basic human decency or laws and regulations designed to protect the common welfare, a courageous follower should consider the following gradations of response:

> The first incident or suggestion of violating basic human values, or skirting laws and regulations consistent with these values, must be energetically challenged at the level it occurs, or at higher levels as necessary, using all the tools available for effectively engaging the leaders.

> If a second incident occurs, the response must be a clear moral statement of intent to withdraw support should the behavior recur in any form. (If, in extreme cases, announcing the intention would jeopardize the follower's physical safety, it is best to proceed as if a third incident had occurred.)

> Begin preparing for the potential need to blow the whistle on the immoral activities by documenting them so that your claims cannot be easily discredited.

> Any further incident should be met by blowing the whistle on the immoral activity through whatever channels are available inside or, if necessary, outside the organization.

> If you cannot obtain documentation or corroboration for all your claims but can for one claim, focus public attention on this point. One irrefutable demonstration of a leader or organization's malfeasance is more powerful than many refutable charges.

Once we publicly disavow the leader's actions, restraints on speech are lifted, and we can communicate more forcefully to a broader audience. Whatever power we possessed by being close to a leader can now be directed to exposing the violation of values we have witnessed or perhaps even contributed to.

This is not a happy juncture as it signals that our loyal efforts to transform the offending behavior have failed. However, if the public actions taken are proportional to the potential for harm to the organization and those whom its actions affect, it is still a courageous act designed to serve the common purpose and core community values.

PROTECTING YOURSELF

As studies of whistleblowers amply demonstrate, it is not uncommon for a follower who disavows or opposes a leader to pay a significant price. If leaders are deeply insecure and vindictive, they may even retaliate for simply suggesting that they review their behavior or policies.

Courageous followers may need to come armed with "weapons" of their own—information, allies, bylaws, legal representation—that make the price of retaliating too high and make cooperating with efforts to reform a situation more attractive. The best protection for abusive leaders is darkness and secrecy; our protection is light and documentation.

Followers are in a stronger position when they are insulated from formal retribution. Public officials appointed for fixed terms, educators with tenure, workers whose union will shield them from retaliatory demotion, staff who have accrued enough years of service for full retirement benefits—all enjoy some protection and are more prone to challenge leadership policies or practices with which they disagree. We would do well to try to create some of this insulation in our own lives. In addition to keeping detailed documentation, contingency plans might include:

> **obtaining strong written references, for use in a future employment search or court proceeding, before publicly opposing a leader;**
>
> **developing media relations who will be interested in our story when we are ready to tell it;**

affiliating with groups that will support us emotionally, legally, and financially if we oppose the leader's practices;

making arrangements with friends or relatives to care for our families if a confrontation with the leader risks their physical or emotional safety.

Regardless of contingency arrangements, if we make the decision to publicly blow the whistle, our lives will be severely impacted. We will find ourselves under enormous stress. The least endearing parts of our personality may become more pronounced under this stress. At the time we most need support, we may drive it away.

It is important to emotionally prepare ourselves and our support system. We need to confide in our family, friends, and colleagues. We need to give them a chance to be part of our decision-making process. When we call on them to stand by us, they will not feel they are being dragged into something without consultation. We must ground ourselves in the deepest sense of purpose and the highest values we have, so that we can face whatever ordeal awaits us with grace rather than bitterness.

WHEN LEADERS MUST BE OPPOSED

There is a large step between disavowing a leader and actively opposing him. When disavowing a leader, a follower is casting light on the leader's actions in the court of public opinion and leaving it to the corrective mechanisms of the organization or society to respond.

When courageous followers choose to actively oppose a leader, they themselves mobilize available mechanisms for disempowering the leader. When attention has been called to corrupt behavior and the corrective mechanisms of society respond too slowly or indifferently, courageous followers may feel responsible for firing them up. The police captain who sadistically beats suspects, the politician who abrogates the legitimate constitution, the executive who orders a toxic waste coverup, the zealot who commits arson to preserve his community's "racial purity"—each deserves to be vigorously opposed.

Of course, there are risks to opposing venality. The obvious risk is retaliation by leaders who are being opposed. There are also psychological risks. Although these will not dissuade courageous followers, we should be aware of them:

> Followers may become obsessed with opposing the leader and expend all their energy on efforts to stop him.

> Followers who become obsessed run the risk of themselves disregarding basic human values in pursuit of their obsession.

> Followers who become obsessed will pay a heavy price in their personal lives, because obsession is the destroyer of balance.

> If followers were victimized by the leader, they may wind up paying twice: once by the victimization and once by the obsession to stop it from happening to others.

> This price may be the cost of disempowering evil, but it is a greater victory if followers pursue their goal with determination rather than obsession.

> The antidote to obsession is generating as much energy toward the positive ideals we are trying to realize as toward the source of evil we are trying to stop.

A good example of a vigorous and balanced opposition to evil is an organization in the southern United States that was created to prevent the resurgence of Ku Klux Klan–type groups, which had terrorized racial and ethnic minorities in the past. The organization recognized that it was becoming obsessed with exposing neofascist leaders and their hate groups. In order to create a healthy balance to its aggressive litigation program, it initiated a project to teach tolerance in schools throughout the country and has sustained this as a key part of its focus.

If a follower's opposition is balanced, energetic, skillful, and timely, she can become the catalyst that triggers society's mechanisms for broadly exposing the abuse and preventing its recurrence. At this point, the follower has transformed herself and become an opposition leader.

The most difficult and dangerous situation occurs when the abuse of power is violent and society's legal mechanisms for correcting it have been corrupted by the abusers. Opposition must be bold and imaginative to counter the use of violent force by mobilizing the overwhelming force of public opinion against it. Communications media, which can almost instantaneously mobilize large numbers of people and focus the whole world's attention on an abuse of power, appears to be shifting the advantage to such opposition.

The gravest choice a courageous follower turned opposition leader makes is whether to use force to counter force in political situations in which democratic processes have been abrogated. By doing so, there is a risk of escalating violence and suffering. Nonviolent resistance has always been a brave and morally unimpeachable response. But can we condemn the followers who tried to stop Hitler's carnage by concealing a bomb in a briefcase under the table at which Hitler sat? Few of us would condemn that act. We mourn that it failed! But it is rare when the case is so clear-cut. Using violence to counter violence is a terrible, slippery slope. In almost all cases it, too, becomes abusive—the ultimate lose-lose situation.

When followers morally oppose violent leaders while those leaders are still vulnerable, they have an opportunity to preempt situations becoming so desperate that they must entertain opposing violent force with like force.

EVIL BEHAVIOR

Any behavior falls somewhere along a spectrum of intensity for that type of activity. The study of statistics tells us that the distribution of intensities within a group always forms a familiar bell-shaped curve. Most people display similar intensity and form the top of the bell. Diminishing numbers display lesser or greater intensities as we move toward the extremes. About 2.5 percent approach each extreme, and less than 0.2 percent fall within either extreme itself.

Thus, most people are "averagely" good or bad, a handful stand out in either direction, and a tiny few are saintly or bedeviled. Because we so rarely encounter such extreme behavior, we may discount it. On the good-evil spectrum, we do so at great peril. As rare as it may be, extremely evil behavior does exist, and if not recognized and dealt with for what it is, it will cause great suffering.

Evil acts are devoid of empathy for the harm done to others. They are only concerned with what the perpetrator gets out of the act materially or psychologically. There have been many attempts to explain the root of evil, but we seem no closer now to understanding or eradicating its roots than were ancient cultures. We can, however, observe the manifestations of evil and act to stop its progression. A leader who is allowed to act narcissistically with indifference to the harm caused to others is on a trajectory toward evil behavior.

Leaders who commit evil acts usually mask them from the broader public until they accumulate enough power to flaunt the behavior with impunity. Thus, fighting evil is like fighting a fire. It is better to contain it early than to wait until it is out of control and consuming everything in its path. Evil is best fought from within an organization by courageous followers close enough to the leader to see behind the public mask. We are the firebreak.

Conversely, evil is fanned by followers who abandon their empathy with the suffering of others, either through fear or through seduction by a leader's twisted vision. Followers who commit evil acts are not necessarily evil people. There is often powerful pressure for followers to commit these acts. Implicitly or explicitly, they have been promised personal gain for conforming and threatened with personal harm for not conforming. Because their peers are under the same pressure, these acts begin to appear normal. They are even characterized as moral by the leadership through an inverted values logic. This is how millions of people came to support a Ku Klux Klan, a Nazi regime, or other brutal movements. It is also how egregious white-collar crimes or official coverups that require the collusion of numbers of people occur. We must be vigilant against starting down the slippery slope of evil behavior:

> **The very first time we are pressured to commit an evil act, we will experience discomfort; an inner voice protests against it.**

> **We must listen to this inner voice and recognize that it is more valid than the voice of our peers or leader, regardless of the language in which they wrap their demands, and with profound courage we must draw a line then and there.**

If we do not listen to this inner voice, it will speak again when we actually commit the act; it may even scream in revulsion.

This may be our last opportunity to listen to the voice; if we do not listen now, we will need to smother it, anesthetize ourselves, and deny our deeds in order to live with them.

At that point we will become indistinguishable from an evil person.

Many wrong acts are not evil. They are done out of clashing values, misplaced priorities, ignorance, or insensitivity. Do not hastily label acts as evil. Doing so can devalue the very concept of evil. It can also be self-righteous and self-serving and itself become a justification for evil behavior.

But, when confronted with actual evil behavior, especially within our own organization or movement, we must not rationalize it, must not hide in the false safety of the group, must not stifle our internal protests in the silence of our peers. If we underestimate evil, it will engulf us. If we behave normally in its presence, it will turn our lives upside down.

We must expose the behavior against standards of basic human decency with the brightest searchlight we can find or build. The less fortunate parts of the world continue to be littered with the corpses of those who were the victims of evil behavior. In more "civilized" societies, demagogues, charlatans, and bullies damage thousands of lives in subtler destructive ways. If we cannot help the perpetrators of these acts restrain and transform their behavior, we must use our power to expose and isolate them.

Fortunately, it is very rare that we will find ourselves in this situation. When we do, let us hope we have the courage to act.

IF WE DECIDE TO STAY

Despite the moral demand to leave, a follower may choose to stay—the price of leaving may simply be too high. Courage is not absolute. We cannot judge another for making this choice unless we ourselves have faced it.

If we decide to stay, we may justify our decision on the grounds that if all the "moderate" people in the organization left, it would only become more extreme and harmful. There is some functional truth to this perspective. It can require courage to remain in an organization whose values we do not share and whose excesses we intend to curb. It is a very unpleasant experience to continue dealing with people whose style and activities we abhor. But if our departure leaves them freer to abuse power, a moral argument can be made for staying.

If we make the choice to stay, we must be prepared for several things:

We must accept moral and legal responsibility for the tacit or actual support we are giving to the abuse.

We can never claim before a legal or moral court that "we had no choice."

We must take incremental action at every opportunity to diminish the abuses and the impact they have on their victims.

We must take bold action to reform the organization when the moment for change presents itself and our stand can make a difference.

In more typical situations, people often stay despite a discomfort with the current leadership. They calculate that, for a variety of reasons, the tenure of the current leadership is limited. They are hopeful that its successors will be more compatible with their own philosophy or style and that the situation will correct itself. In the interim, they do what they can to forward the common purpose.

In extreme situations, this "wait it out" strategy may not be viable. The decision to stay as a moderating force is filled with as much risk as the decision to leave. It is the equivalent of becoming a "fifth column" in hostile territory. The follower who chooses to stay in these circumstances may pay with peace of mind or worse.

As is true for all moral decisions, the decision to stay in the face of morally unacceptable behavior must be made with as much honesty about one's own motivations and actions as about the actions of others. The courage to take moral action of any type in full knowledge of its attendant risks is the mark of significant development as a human being. Whatever the consequences of one's actions, when they are faced with one's integrity intact, moral behavior has already won.

7

THE COURAGE TO SPEAK TO THE HIERARCHY

WE HAVE EXAMINED AN IDEAL relationship between followers and leaders from many perspectives. Virtually everything discussed rests on the assumption that the individual who is in the follower role has earned the trust of the leader by reason of good works. This, in turn, assumes access to the leader and having formed at least a professional, if not a personal, relationship with the leader.

In practice, in large institutions, government agencies, and corporations, the vast majority of staff, let alone the constituents these organizations serve, do not have direct relationships with the senior leaders. Can the principles of courageous followership apply across these levels?

In the coaching and training I conduct in complex organizations with many tiers of management, this is a crucial question. It is true that the relationship we have with our direct supervisor often has the most bearing on our day-to-day work satisfaction. But our deeper sense of organizational well-being is affected by our perceptions of how clearly the higher strata of leaders are aware of the realities of the organization. Do they know what we experience from our vantage point as they seek to guide the organization toward our common future? Or are they victims of the bubble that forms around senior leaders and filters out the experience of those who have their "boots on the ground"? Too often, there is a sense that senior leaders do not sufficiently grasp these realities or the impact of their own initiatives. The response to this perception is often disappointment, dismay, and cynicism. None of these is the response of a courageous follower.

What are the alternatives? In this chapter we look at a special application of courageous follower behaviors to situations in which the leader is far removed from the follower by reason of hierarchy. We are addressing the need to ensure that senior leaders have sufficient and accurate data on which to base decisions, as well as the desire of "corporate citizens" to see that their organization is well cared for by offering their professional perspectives in meaningful ways to the leaders who set organization direction.

Those who work in large organizations know that this is much easier said than done. On a pragmatic level, senior leaders can digest just so much information. Thus the information that wends its way up multiple levels to the top of the hierarchy is generally condensed and recondensed. In the process, those who believe they know what their senior leaders like and don't like to hear, will spin, scrub, summarize, and sanitize the reports.

On a personal-political level, the intermediaries who occupy the relay points upward may be concerned that data and analysis that are too raw and frank may harm the perception of their own competence. Are they not expected to manage and eliminate problems before they reach the levels above them? Ideally, yes. Realistically, they cannot always do so. In these cases, the impulse to soften the adverse realities conveyed upward is strong. Approval processes designed for efficiency are instead used for image and perception management.

Even when there are opportunities for personnel at lower ranks to directly report reality as they see it to senior leaders, cultural mechanisms can interfere with the process. Hierarchical *structure* serves a very valid function of clarifying who can commit the organization to large endeavors and the costs required for them. In contrast, culturally defined rules of hierarchical *relationships* can interrupt the transmission of important information and perspectives. How does this work?

Hierarchical structure is almost inevitable in complex human endeavors. At its most profound level it is the social antidote to continuous and debilitating conflict within a group. An individual or governing body is formally empowered to choose between competing values, options, and interests. Even in organizations that are essentially twenty-first-century networks that work largely on egalitarian principles, a measure of hierarchical structure always emerges to facilitate the work of the organization.

Hierarchical relationships are the internalized and often unspoken rules of behavior between those of different stations in the system. They are fraught with potential barriers to the candor needed for senior leaders to receive the data and analysis that good decision making requires. A case

in point was my own reaction to authority that I reported in the introduction to Chapter 1 when I became uncomfortable in the presence of
prominent leaders. What caused this? Some internal programming
seemed to activate and adversely affect the ease I normally experience
with people.

It does not take much to imagine how such programming occurs. We
are social beings living within the great variety of cultures and subcultures
of humanity. We must socialize our young to participate in the settings in
which they will live. In contemporary society, this includes the family unit,
all levels of school, sports, youth clubs, religious observance, and the work
environments in which they will find themselves. For many, it also includes
military service. To function at every stage, youth must learn appropriate
respect for authority: parents, caregivers, teachers, coaches, referees,
prelates, law enforcement officers, and, ultimately, workplace supervisors.
The social penalties for not learning these lessons sufficiently are severe.
Sometimes in this process, the respect for authority is learned too well.

In my talks with senior executives in sensitive operations such as intelligence or nuclear security, I am struck by how many are unfamiliar with
the social science research on conformity and obedience. This research
relates directly to the capacity of their staff to be candid in expressing
divergent views to their own. For example, the famous experiments conducted by Dr. Stanley Milgram in the mid-twentieth century, and widely
replicated by others, demonstrate that two-thirds of people will comply
with authority even when they are deeply uncomfortable about doing so
as the orders they are given appear to be causing grievous harm. They

comply though no duress is being exerted on them to do so. They are simply responding to the trappings of authority, which in the experiments consist of nothing more than a lab coat, a clipboard, and a statement that "the experiment requires that you continue." This is our evidence of how deep the programming is regarding authority.

When we work on a regular basis with a direct supervisor, some of this programming is loosened by the human relationship that naturally develops. Without the frequency of contact that occurs with our direct supervisor, the programming can retain far greater force toward more elevated superiors. Competent professionals can experience considerable anxiety when called on to brief the head of their department, let alone when the need arises to question a problematic belief held by that leader. Candor and appropriate assertiveness often suffer in the strain of the encounter. Yet that same department head who inadvertently triggered this anxiety may, in turn, report to leaders several levels above him and experience similar trepidation. We begin to see the obstacles that candid data and analysis face in their labored swim upstream.

Some observers of these dynamics hypothesize they are changing in younger generations due to the weakening role of parental authority in shaping behavior and the increasingly strong role of peer relations. Perhaps this will be borne out in future studies, but we cannot yet devalue the considerable effect of hierarchy and authority on behavior. This chapter will explore strategies and techniques for overcoming the internal and external barriers to conveying information and perspectives effectively across hierarchical levels.

THE CHALLENGE OF MANY HANDS

Life is simple when lived in very small units. You make a decision, act on it, and live with the consequences of your decision. But small units cannot create the same marvels generated by large numbers of well-organized, educated, financed, and coordinated human beings. Life gets complex in larger units, and ways to organize this complexity emerge.

Some approaches are organic, such as the thrilling world of self-organizing groups that utilize the power of networks rather than hierarchies. Even here, though, when competing views within the group create an impasse, or evidence of unfair practices emerge, additional rules become necessary. Largely, the community itself ferrets out antisocial behavior and enforces adherence to its rules through social pressure. But at some point a formal authority must emerge that acts as arbiter while respecting the group's values.

There is little question that self-organizing networks are spreading, over-laying, and connecting the massive hierarchies that have permitted the creation of the knowledge, wealth, and governance at our current stage of human development. But, like the evolution of human culture itself, old structures and technologies endure alongside emerging ones for prolonged periods. If hierarchies are ever destined to be replaced by networks, this will not occur for a considerable time, though they will surely be improved by them.

Both networks and large hierarchies have the inherent characteristic of "many hands" touching the same piece of work. There are important qualitative differences, however. Instead of the near real-time dialogue networks can achieve, hierarchies tend to communicate linearly. Data may be widely accessible, but analytic reports about that data tend to move step by step up the rungs. What is done with the report at each level can preserve or dilute its power. Material changes can be made that distort its meaning without the preparer being consulted. Or it can cycle back to the preparer multiple times with requests to soften the findings, requests that feel difficult to refuse.

While this process is occurring, in complex organizations the report typically travels on simultaneous tracks to other functions that are affected by it for comment, and to bureaucratic checkpoints for oversight of legality, budget ramifications, public relations issues, and the like. So many hands touch and make changes to the report that it becomes impractical to hold the originator responsible for its final shape.

Studies of how to achieve accountability in such environments show that many mechanisms can be put in place, but, ultimately, none is fully successful. It always come down, at some point, to an individual in the organization being caring, courageous, and skillful enough to take ownership of the report and the decisions that it will engender. The task then is to find a way to alert senior decision makers to the data and their meaning before the decision makers commit the organization to a course that will be difficult and painful to change. At times, you may be that individual. If so, your first task is to divest yourself of the tempting excuse of "many hands" to avoid assuming this responsibility.

A contributing factor to be aware of to help free ourselves from this excuse is the phenomenon known as *learned helplessness*. When experimental subjects are repeatedly unable to discover a way to reduce or eliminate a source of pain, they cease trying. They remain this way even when new options for dealing with the source of pain are introduced into the experiment. They have learned to feel helpless even when they are no longer helpless. Time spent in complex bureaucracies is prone to infect any of us with a dose of learned helplessness. The antidote is remembering that the present is not the same as the past. We can ask ourselves questions such as these that focus on important distinctions:

> "What threats or opportunities are emerging that, if well articulated, will capture the attention of the organization's leaders?"

> "What options for courses of action to recommend exist now that did not exist earlier?"

> "What new channels of communication are available for reaching senior leaders?"

> "What influential networks can I now access that would be helpful in stating the case?"

> "Where is the lever that can now be pulled?"

> "What am I going to do about it?"

One pair of committed hands, at a critical time and place, can provide the balance that rights a hierarchy that is tipping in an ill-advised direction when incomplete, manipulated, or misinterpreted data threaten to generate poor or dangerous decisions.

DOING THE HOMEWORK

We see something wrong in the organization: a policy that is not working, a program being implemented over fierce resistance, a lack of focus, inadequate funding of strategic activities, rules that frustrate stakeholders, golden opportunities not being pursued . . . the list can be long.

Our impulse is to send our observations up the command channel with the implication that higher-ups should fix this. We mention our observations at a meeting, send an anxious message, or draft a short memo.

Nothing happens.

We do this from time to time on a variety of issues. An edge creeps into our communication. The edge is the alienated attitude we are developing. Aren't senior leaders paid to see and address the very things we see that are wrong and in need of their attention?

From the leaders' perspective, of course, there may be more important things to tend to at this time. They would not be leading if they always set priorities based on others' views. In the logic of hierarchies, we are being both tunnel-visioned and guilty of upward or reverse delegation.

But what if we are right? What if the matter we are calling to their attention is as important to the overall well-being of the organization as the issues that they are currently treating as priority?

Underneath this common breakdown between levels of the hierarchy is the distinction between a complaint and a serious issue analysis. Both seem to be calling a problem to the attention of upper management, but only one is actionable in the form upper management receives it.

A *complaint* takes the form of a few sentences or paragraphs that say, in effect, "Here is what I see happening. I don't think this is right. Something should be done about it."

You may argue this is not inherently a complaint, but rather data and an expression of concern. But its structure is similar to that of a complaint.

It conveys an impression of something wrong, not an analysis of the situation, its causes, and potential solutions. It is an implicit demand that someone else take responsibility for the situation, presumably the leader.

An *issue analysis* provides information in an actionable form—for example:

> A preliminary issue description and request for a meeting to elaborate on its potential consequences and possible resolutions

> A problem statement with preliminary data attached and a request for authorization to form a task force to explore policy options

> An executive summary supported by full data charts, pros and cons of alternative courses of action, recommendations that upper management can approve, and a commitment to plan the execution.

Too often we think we have made a recommendation that can be acted on when we have really just lodged a complaint. Why do we do this? In part for the same reason that senior leaders have not addressed the issue. We are already so busy with our defined responsibilities that we cannot give the other matter the attention it requires. In effect, we are prioritizing it in a similar way to how the leader is prioritizing it, whether either of us is doing so consciously. Recognizing this distinction can restore our identification with the leader and our sense of partnership.

Does this mean courageous followers never point out issues they do not have time to analyze? That would be very dangerous. We offer our observations but do not mistake them for analyses on which leaders should unquestionably act.

If the issue is truly one of great importance, we need to make time to present it professionally and compellingly. If our workload precludes doing this, we need to make the case for being relieved of other responsibilities in order to focus on the issue or for assigning others to address it who have sufficient capacity to do so.

Once given responsibility for an issue, those assigned to the task almost always address it professionally. The mark of the courageous follower is not waiting to be assigned the task before generating the initial analysis and recommendations on which leaders can act.

FRAMING THE ISSUE TO
COMMAND ATTENTION

It really is difficult to focus the attention of very senior leaders on things that they have not asked for. They are tightly scheduled and preoccupied with many issues that have significant consequences.

If the matter we wish to bring to their attention is clearly related to their established priorities, it makes the task easier. Of course, virtually any issue can be construed to impact strategic goals, so leaders tend to get inured to every argument being positioned this way.

If the matter is sufficiently important to raise it several echelons, there is essentially one of two reasons for doing so: there is either significant downside risk attached to it or significant upside potential. These are the matters that, in a sense, are the proper focus of senior leadership. They represent the extremes of what can derail the leaders' vision or make significant strides toward achieving it.

Before we proceed, we need to acknowledge a fact of life. While a leader's vision should always embrace the organization's mission, it also embraces the leader's own welfare and future. Except for the rare saints among us, we all operate on self-interest as well as the common good. As long as self-interest does not overshadow the common good, this motivation is not a problem. When we present the downside risk or upside potential to a situation, most leaders create their own link between these and their professional reputation and personal welfare. In hierarchies, the top leaders are inextricably identified with results or lack of results, and with the triumphs and embarrassments of the organization. This fact reinforces their attention to downside risk and upside potential. If the issue we are raising affects these matters, we should be able to get a hearing.

> "I am requesting this meeting because the data I have looked at demonstrate significant financial exposure that should be brought to your attention."

> "I believe this matter deserves your attention because, with a slight alteration of strategy, we are well positioned to make the greatest advance in our twenty-year history."

That leaders focus on risk and opportunity also poses a challenge for courageous followers. Leaders in many environments are more prone to focus on upside potential than downside risk. That is where the glory lies. If not for this bias toward risk, enormous projects like the laying of transcontinental railroads or encircling the globe with communications satellites would never be accomplished. The capacity for appropriate risk is inherent in leadership. Courageous followers recognize and honor this characteristic.

At the same time, the bias toward achieving memorable legacies can blind leaders to potentially catastrophic risk. The odds of the downside risk materializing are often small. The magnitude of the upside potential is alluring. In business, this tendency is magnified by the personal financial rewards associated with success. In these situations, even a clear demonstration of the potential for catastrophic risk may fail to move senior leaders. The line between courageous risk taker and compulsive gambler can blur. This is especially problematic if the risk the leader is taking comes on the heels of a string of successes: the gambler feels charmed, and those like the board, with authority to rein in the risk, are silenced by fear of jeopardizing the winning streak. At this point the stars are aligned for potential catastrophe.

Sometimes, the best a courageous follower can do in this situation is to frame the issue in terms of risk containment.

> **"I encourage you to establish a task force to examine the risks in our strategy and identify ways of reducing the exposure we have currently."**

> **"The rewards for success in this initiative are tremendous. It would be prudent to reduce the risks by taking the following three actions."**

If the risks appear too great for this equivocation, the opposite approach is in order, which might be described as goal containment.

> **"Though the chances of failure are relatively small, the extent of the potential damage is so great that it could ruin the company brand or destroy the company itself. Therefore, we recommend**

a course change that still preserves many of the goals for which you are striving."

"The potential for [reputational, political, financial] damage is so severe that it could create widespread backlash and even be career ending. Therefore, we urge you to consider the following modifications that scale back the initiative."

Either approach would be presented with rigorous analysis and as much political support as could be lined up in advance. The very act of putting the potential risk on the record can be sufficient to cause a leader to pause and reconsider the matter.

Ideally, a courageous follower would also find breakthrough ideas with significant upside potential to bring to the attention of senior leaders. We need to say yes or "Here's how to reach your goals" more than we say no or "That won't work." If we only raise the prospect of risk, there is danger of becoming the organizational Cassandra, the legendary figure who correctly warned of pending doom and remained unheeded.

EDUCATING THE HIERARCHY

A seismic shift has occurred in many organizational structures. The deepest knowledge in the organization no longer resides at its top echelons but is embedded in the middle and bottom. The more that organizations become collections of knowledge workers, the more leaders are dependent on their followers to help them understand the threats and opportunities that reside in continuously emerging and evolving technologies and social and environmental trends.

In many organizations, the highest ranks of leadership are filled with professionals who came up through finance, marketing, legal, or public affairs tracks. They bring important skill sets but not a command of technical and operational issues. Those who did come up through technical tracks may no longer have sufficient hands-on connection to their field to be on the creative edge. They need to be continuously educated by those below them if they are to make well-informed decisions.

There is often a generational reversal of roles in this educational process. Leaders have power over the machinery of the hierarchy, but it is the younger followers' world they are trying to influence. The new patterns of thinking and possibility that exist in this world must be integrated into the mental maps of the organization's leaders. Older patterns, which effectively served battle-tested veterans, need to be reevaluated or even unlearned. This is not an activity that works well by being passed up a hierarchy one level at a time. Too much is lost in translation. The entire hierarchy needs direct exposure to new ways of thinking.

In a world of continuous and rapid change, a portion of every leader's day is of necessity spent learning on the job, making sense out of shifting patterns, and constructing strategies to take advantage of new developments. Knowledgeable staff are pulled from the middle or lower levels of the hierarchy to brief leaders in their areas of expertise. Followers must become comfortable teaching those at the top of the hierarchy, keeping these guidelines in mind:

> Be well prepared and confident in what you know.

> Be economical and clear in how you present it.

> Define all terms you are using.

> Recognize that you are assuming a leadership role in transmitting knowledge and you are responsible for others being able to follow.

> Don't get thrown by demonstrations of impatience or confusion by the formal leaders—these often accompany the struggle to form new frameworks of understanding.

> Ask questions that help the leaders engage with the material they need to understand better.

> Don't move on to your next point without achieving clarity.

> Invite those in the meeting who do seem to understand to help create the needed clarity for others.

The quality of decisions that have a large impact will depend on the quality of understanding that skilled followers engender in their leaders and the speed with which they do so.

CIRCUMVENTING THE HIERARCHY

If you need to bring something to the attention of an executive two or three levels above you, in most cultures it is expected that you will first bring it to the attention of your immediate supervisor. Normally this protocol presents no problem.

At times, however, you will encounter the dilemma of immediate supervisors or managers not being willing conduits for your information, ideas, or concerns. In the case of reporting serious risk, they may not be as certain as you are of your assessment and feel leery of throwing cold water on a leader's passion for a bold initiative. In the case of suggesting upside potential, they may not fully grasp your ideas and don't want to be seen as promoting an initiative they regard as having dubious merit.

Assuming that your concerns or ideas are well thought out, we now enter the terrain of potentially bypassing levels of the hierarchy. What is the calculus of whether it is worth circumventing command channels?

In some cultures, the answer is simple: do it. The culture supports a free flow of upward communication. Courtesy only requires copying your direct supervisors on written communication or advising them of oral conversations. No offense is intended or taken.

In many other cultures, the decision is not as simple. The value placed on respecting the hierarchy is strong or even fierce. Contemporary research suggests that in more than half the cases of circumvention, there is adverse impact on the relationship with immediate supervisors. What may be surprising, however, is that this is true in only slightly more than half the cases. The rest of the time the action of circumvention does not affect the relationship and in some cases even strengthens it. Why is this so?

In cases where followers do their homework well and report useful and important information and suggestions, leaders tend to signal their approval. If the follower has provided the data and ideas without casting aspersion on intermediary supervisors, leaders don't usually question why they aren't hearing from those supervisors directly. It is the data and ideas that are important. Supervisors may even benefit indirectly from the credit given to the alertness of their staff.

If the follower had the courage to raise the matter with senior executives despite the more cautious stance of supervisors, her stature may be enhanced in the eyes of the supervisors. In the future, those supervisors will tend to regard her as someone to heed, both for her perspicacity and for her determination. She achieves a certain acceptance as a partner because of her demonstrated commitment to serving the mission and willingness to challenge the culture if needed to serve that mission well.

Are there ways to improve the odds that a decision to circumvent the hierarchy will not damage relationships? Being scrupulous on certain points will help:

> Unless the situation contains immediate danger or presents a fleeting window of opportunity, research and prepare your case well.

> Identify peers to act as sounding boards for the case you will present, and incorporate their feedback into your presentation.

> Give your chain of command the opportunity to digest and support your intention to raise the issue higher.

> If you cannot gain their support, assure them that you will accept responsibility for any negative outcomes of your actions.

> Do not let resentment about lack of support from supervisors bleed into your presentation to senior management.

> If your ideas are well received, be gracious in your success.

> Ask your supervisors how you could do a better job in the future of presenting your reasons for wanting to raise a matter up the hierarchy.

When circumventing the hierarchy seems necessary, we need to be cautious about falling into hierarchical relationship traps. We cannot let the internalized rules of our superiors regarding the supposed sacredness of the hierarchy, versus the true sacredness of the mission, silence us. Just as important, we must be aware of and manage our own internalized rules. If our professional or personal sense of responsibility calls for us to speak up, we cannot let rules about being well-behaved boys and girls keep us from doing so. But we must be equally mindful that we don't fall into the countervailing rule set of rebellious adolescents. There are ways to do what must be done respectfully. In consequential circumstances, we need to take consequential actions. *How* we do so can make all the difference.

SPEAKING UP IN MULTILEVEL MEETINGS

At times we find ourselves in situations in which the hierarchy is all present in a room or around a real or virtual table. In very well-led groups, conscious efforts are made to reduce the dampening effect of hierarchical differences on candor and participation. But far from all groups succeed in creating an egalitarian dialogue. The rules of hierarchical relationships, though unstated, hang thickly over the exchange.

In many cultures, this is a situation fraught with delicacy. There are two basic permutations to the sensitivities. The first is when the most senior leader around the table expresses a strong view that is not supported by the data available to the hierarchy of followers who are present. The most junior follower may want to raise concerns about the leader's view, but her own superiors in the meeting are not doing so. Their silence makes the follower's intention to speak appear more questionable or imprudent. The second situation is perhaps even more dangerous to relationships. The follower's direct superior has expressed a view that is not supported by the follower's data. Should the follower risk embarrassing her supervisor by correcting his data or risk leaving the most senior leader with an incorrect impression that could lead to a poor decision?

These questions are not difficult to answer if the culture understands that the highest loyalty must be to the common purpose. But in the "real" world, loyalty to your direct superiors is often a coequal requirement. Thus, strategies are needed for satisfying the requirements, or at least not flagrantly violating them.

The first rule in situations where several levels in the chain of command are present is: *don't embarrass anyone.*

When professionalism requires you to present divergent data or perspectives, do so mindfully. Steven L. Katz, a management consultant who has both worked in the White House and studied many of the world's best professional lion tamers (actual, not figurative, lions), reminds us that when working with a group of senior leaders, you are interacting with the equivalent of a pride of lions. Each lion knows its standing in the pride. Their sense of security depends on that standing being respected. If lions feel their position challenged, they will strike out at the challenger. Body language, choice of words, and tone of delivery become extremely important in this situation. Surprising superiors with an unexpected and unwelcome move, or forcefully challenging their ideas in front of the other lions, will win you little support and more often a good cuffing or worse. Appropriate deference to their position in "the pride" without weakening your own presence or contribution is both artful and crucial.

> **"Sir, you are making a good point. There is some additional data that may warrant our reconsidering that conclusion."**

> **"_____ [the follower's manager who is present at the table] has offered a potential solution. I need to apologize that I was not able to brief him prior to the meeting on new developments that may change our thinking."**

> **"With your [the highest leader's] and _____'s [your direct supervisor's] permission, I'd like to present additional information that may be relevant to your decision."**

You can also couch a point using the socially acceptable device of asking to "play devil's advocate." This is a linguistic package that conveys "There may be another way to look at this that could avoid unforeseen trouble." If not overused, it tends to help the leaders and group accept the divergent perspective as good group process rather than as a personal challenge.

> **"With the group's permission, may I play devil's advocate?"**

> **"If I may play devil's advocate for a moment, what would happen if . . . ?"**

In a multilevel meeting, the twin enemies of good decision making threaten to converge: the conformity and blind spots engendered by groupthink, and the self-censorship stemming from internalized hierarchical rules.

A voice that combines diplomacy and candor can make a crucial difference in these settings

FINDING FORMAL PLATFORMS
OF INFLUENCE

When trying to influence the upper echelons of a large hierarchal organization, operating as a lone voice may not carry sufficient weight, regardless of the merits of your perspective. There are too many voices and too many issues. Your message can easily get lost in the din. This can be remedied by finding or creating a platform from which to speak.

All large organizations have numerous internal working groups established to improve the organization. Becoming an active member of a group whose mandate would allow it to address the issues of concern to you opens up communication and influence channels.

This strategy requires the willingness to assume additional responsibilities beyond your core work. It also requires becoming a genuine asset to the working group. Joining solely to ram through "your issue" may generate as much resistance as trying to push the message upward.

In some cases, the right group for championing the issue doesn't yet exist. In this case, the act of courageous followership dovetails into an act of peer leadership as you encourage the formation of such a group. Most leaders will be supportive and appreciative of such an effort if they sense it is being done in good faith.

When these groups are ready to report up to the hierarchy, they must take full advantage of the platform they have. The presentation must have impact proportional to the importance of the message. Senior leaders live through a parade of daily briefings. A "corporate language" develops that is professional, familiar, and expected. For many messages, this approach is sufficient. It does not serve the leader, organization, or messenger well to inflate the importance of an issue. But, if the risk or opportunity is truly of the first order of magnitude, using the modulated corporate tone can fatally devalue the message.

The challenge of conveying risk or opportunity upward through channels is that it gets diluted as it passes through intermediaries. In contrast, a senior-level briefing is an opportunity to directly transmit the gravity of risk or potential of an opportunity. At this juncture, courageous followers must let their authentic, powerful voice permeate through the layers of their own internal rule sets toward authority and the "don't make waves" voice expected in many organization cultures.

> "You see from the data the potentials in the situation. It would be easy for us to discount the chance of failure. That would be a serious mistake because we would all share culpability for proceeding in the face of severe risks."

> "We understand the initiative we are proposing departs from current strategy. Nevertheless, we recommend starting a demonstration project immediately. If successful, this new direction will ensure our viability for years to come."

Other platforms, not of our own making, at times present themselves. Leaders periodically reach into an organization through all-hands "town hall" meetings to provide information, quell concerns, or seek buy-in for new strategy. Or, they may invite groups of a dozen or two employees to lunch without middle managers present in an attempt to stay real about what is happening in the organization.

At these types of skip-level meetings, two extremes can occur that are counterproductive. At one extreme, employees sit on their hands and do not speak up about their concerns for the organization. At the other, intensive venting creates a hostile environment in which leaders become defensive and tune out the message. In either case, the opportunity to speak up to the hierarchy is squandered.

If a collective silence ensues, the most effective act of courageous followership may be to speak directly to this reaction, thereby priming the pump for meaningful exchange:

> "I am aware that many of us hold important views and may not feel comfortable expressing them. I believe our leaders are here in good faith to learn what is holding this organization back. So I am going to be candid, and I encourage my colleagues to be as well."

Such a statement, followed by direct, candid observations and constructive suggestions, sets a tone and standard for others to follow, while putting the leadership on alert to live up to the belief in their good faith.

If there is a crescendo of anger being hurled at the leaders, a calming voice is needed. In the face of churning emotions, this response, too, requires courage and skill.

> "There is a lot of justifiable anger. It was important that our leaders heard the intensity of feelings that exist. It would be productive now to hear constructive ideas on how to move forward. Let me take a stab at offering one idea."

Courageous followership always has the goal of creating adult-to-adult relationships in which both leaders and followers interact as mature professionals. Restoring a tone of mutual responsibility for problem solving is essential. Sometimes, a courageous follower is the best person in the room to model this behavior.

USING INFORMAL PLATFORMS OF INFLUENCE

Platforms also exist between the spaces of the formal organization and on its periphery. Sometimes these are the only platforms available to a courageous follower who has been unsuccessful at using the organization's formal platforms to influence the hierarchy.

Traditionally, informal platforms have been connections with individuals at different levels of the hierarchy formed during activities in which the relational effects of hierarchy were lessened. These activities might include task forces, business travel, organization retreats, or life overlaps such as at schools or volunteer functions. Informal relationships make informal access to the executive easier for skip-channel sharing of information, ideas, and concerns. The real world of human relations works this way, whatever the organizational chart shows. Though useful at critical junctures for serving the common purpose, one must remain mindful of the potential consequences to other relationships of promoting an agenda in this informal manner.

Some traditional avenues for skip-level communications diminish in organizations and projects in which team members are not geographically colocated: the proverbial water cooler, the cafeteria, the softball team are lost. Compensating for this loss are the many opportunities created by the prevalence of distributed electronic communication.

In addition to knowledge sharing, the power of electronically connected individuals and communities of interest to shape opinion is a force to be reckoned with. It is not difficult for disaffected followers to tell their tale widely and build sympathy for it, whether deserved or not. Because of the power of networked communications to amplify and leverage a follower's voice, it is crucial that voice be used responsibly. It is easy to vent. It is harder to use the tenets of courageous followership to actively support leaders while effectively conveying what they need to hear. The collective dialogue must be clearly in service of the common purpose, not in tearing down the organization that is dedicated to that purpose.

If these multilevel, internal organization discussion forums develop a reputation for candor and constructive ideas, an interesting phenomenon may transpire. Instead of followers having to wrestle with options for going to the top of the hierarchy, the top of the hierarchy may start to drop in on the conversation, if their participation is welcomed by the community. At its best, this reduces the age-old problem of keeping leaders of large enterprises connected to the realities of their front-line personnel without going through layers of intermediaries. Of course, there are caveats.

Is it agreed that leaders will have access to the site?

If so, are they committed to it being a true free speech arena?

Can staff post their thoughts anonymously or use pseudonyms if they choose to do so?

What ground rules are needed to keep the site safe for participants and constructive for the organization?

All the dynamics of cross-level communication come into play. Care must be taken. The principle of "Don't embarrass anyone" remains relevant, up and down. Organizational mistakes should be aired so lessons can be learned, but not in a blaming manner. If supervisors are sensitive to being circumvented, it may be best to alert them to issues you plan to post that are likely to trigger that sensitivity.

These are a radically different set of "norms" from those prevailing in nonorganizational electronic conversation. Participants need to be clear about the distinctions. The atmosphere of free-wheeling discussion sites to which we may be accustomed outside the organization can make the more constrained tone of internal sites seem sterile. It is more useful to understand this difference in terms of the role of etiquette in professional settings. Etiquette in its essence is agreed-on ways of showing mutual respect. It can be thought of as the facilitative rules of hierarchical relationships, as distinct from the prohibitive rules that discourage mature and candid conversation.

Whether or not a self-organizing electronic community becomes a resource for the upper echelons of the hierarchy, it can do its own work of honing the ideas its members will take up the hierarchy through more traditional channels. Concurrently, thoughtful and articulate individuals can create their own electronic platforms that attract viewers from different levels of the hierarchy. In this way, their information and perspectives can percolate outward and upward and enter conversations at all levels.

Another set of challenges arises when we find platforms that span organizations, such as industry or professional association discussion sites. These related sites provide additional benefits such as cross-fertilizing ideas between organizations and validating best practices for the industry. The data from these forums can be used to provide more compelling arguments when speaking up to our own hierarchy. But they also carry risks. Boundaries become blurry. Am I participating as a corporate citizen or as a citizen of my field or both? Although there may be fewer formal guidelines for interorganizational speech, there must be heightened sensitivity to the potential impact on our organization and our relationships.

Knowledge, and thus power, will continue to be further distributed throughout organizations and the broader systems in which they operate. The range of informal platforms from which to speak to the hierarchy and to the world it is there to serve will proliferate. As followers and as leaders, we will need to use these new sources of power wisely.

INFLUENCING THE METRICS
THAT INFLUENCE THOUGHT

It is obviously impossible and unnecessary for the senior echelons of a hierarchy to know everything that is happening within the organization and where the organization interfaces with its constituents or customers. Instead, leaders seek to identify what is critical information to inform their decision making and represent that information through metrics they establish and monitor.

Large organizations invest significant resources in designing the processes to determine what information they should be capturing and monitoring. They appreciate that tracking the right combination of metrics can help the organization understand what is occurring now and what is likely to occur in the near or midterm future.

The best leaders understand, however, that these suites of metrics tell only part of the story. Astute leaders work to supplement their grasp of current and future trends through direct observation, dialogue, investigation, and awareness of the field in which they operate. Nevertheless, the weight placed on hard metrics in decision making, performance review, resource allocation, and compensation packages draws leaders' attention forcefully back to those metrics. This tendency poses certain challenges and opportunities regarding speaking up to the hierarchy.

First is the question of what isn't being measured that could be and should be. Environmentalists know this point all too well. They have been waging a long campaign to ensure that "externalities," meaning in this case the impact of economic activity on the environment, are measured so that the real cost of producing and distributing goods and services are calculated. In organizations in which the actions of senior management seem out of alignment with the needs of stakeholders, a contributing factor may be the lack of metrics that would bring the situation to the leadership's attention. Followers who want to redress organizational misalignment may be most effective by getting involved with the processes that review the metrics the organization tracks and rewards.

The next challenge concerning metrics is based on the concept introduced by the philosopher Alfred Korzybski that "the map is not the territory." When senior executives receive a report (the "map") that a hundred thousand units of a service were provided in a given month, they have a general inkling of what occurred, but they don't know what actually occurred in meaningful detail ("the territory"), although they may think they do. Did those reporting from various parts of the organization define the service uniformly? Were the services provided of acceptable quality? Were consumers led to believe the price of services would dramatically increase, thereby creating a demand that will not exist in future months? Was the staff driven to exhaustion to provide those services, precipitating an exodus of good talent from the organization? When we become aware of important contributing factors to the interpretation of the meaning of a metric, we need to use available channels to help executives come closer to understanding the actual territory. Otherwise, decisions are made based on a materially inaccurate picture of reality.

The challenge most frequently experienced by those lower in the hierarchy relates to the pressure to meet numerical goals for key metrics. The pressure in private sector companies attached to quarterly results is well known. Equal pressure can be exerted in the public sector by political figures who want to demonstrate the effectiveness of their administration in education, crime reduction, and other social goods. In both sectors, monetary and status awards are closely tied to "performance." The pressures can be so great that they throw values out of alignment. A wide range of distortions enters the metric reports, including such travesties as lowering standards to improve graduation rates, redefining "serious crime" downwards, mischaracterizing revenue and expenditures, "smoothing" quarterly results, and, at the extreme, committing outright fraud.

Organizations try to minimize the potential to misrepresent data through a variety of controls. But the failures of these controls are legion. In the final analysis, it requires the integrity and courage of individual staff to stand up to inappropriate pressure to manage perceptions by altering measurements. Examples of how you might preempt or resist this pressure include the following:

> **"Like you, I am disappointed we were not able to make the expected increase in productivity. I have begun an analysis and**

will draft a report for you and the senior management team shortly."

"I know it's important to meet our targets. I can't, however, lower our certification requirements to do so. The report will need to stand, and I'll submit a plan for improving results next month."

"Changing the way we characterize quarterly results will mask the underlying situation. This is a realistic picture that we need to address at its root causes."

A strong focus on making well-thought-out targets that promote the organization's mission and welfare are part of effective leadership. Committed followers support these efforts. They use metrics to help themselves as well as their leaders understand what is working that should be reinforced and what is in need of remedy.

In contrast, sending the message "I don't care how you make the target—just do it!" is not values-based leadership. Courageous followers, at whatever level of a hierarchy, resist the pressure to manipulate metrics, even at their own expense. They hold their ground in ensuring accurate data is reported upward, knowing that this gives senior management a better picture of "the territory" on which to take action. Meanwhile, they energetically work to find the causes of disappointing performance, remedy it, and report better news when that is an accurate reflection of the situation.

PATIENCE, PERFORMANCE, AND PERSISTENCE

Courageous followers are naturally doers. They assume responsibility for the common purpose and act within their authority to forward the mission. When working in large hierarchies, it is not unusual to experience frustration at the difficulty of getting those higher up to see what we see, at getting colleagues to generate coordinated solutions, and at getting the organization to change when there is a compelling need to do so.

In the face of these "headwinds," our first responsibility is to maintain our own commitment, energy level, and hopeful outlook. Our attitude is infectious. We can affect those up and down the hierarchy. We are aware of the deficiencies and challenges the organization faces; we do not hide or deny these. But neither do we dwell on these or succumb to cynicism. We feed what is positive in the organization with our own positive energy and support each other in managing the challenges of the organization's shortcomings. We remain empathetic to those at the top of the hierarchy knowing they, too, are coping with significant stresses.

Our second responsibility is to maintain our high level of performance and contribution. We are dedicated to pursuing the mission and serving those the organization exists to serve. Despite barriers and frustrations, we can always find running room to make a contribution. Doing so is both our duty and our sustenance. We have been given the opportunity to serve, and we are serving to our best ability within the existing constraints.

Our third responsibility is to persist in our efforts to improve the organization. Achieving large-scale change in complex organizations is never quick or easy. It may take an entire career to succeed. At times we need to retreat from a stalled attempt and look for a more favorable juncture at which to attract the support of those at the top levels of the hierarchy.

We continue making our contributions to the common purpose and, while doing so, often earn higher positions ourselves in the hierarchy. We gain new platforms from which to influence the direction of the organization and model the changes that are needed.

If, from our elevated position, we remember how the world looks from the lower levels of this journey, we will reach down into the hierarchy for the fresh ideas and energy that are always there and help the best ones rise.

8

THE COURAGE
TO LISTEN TO
FOLLOWERS

WHEN COURAGEOUS FOLLOWERS are successful at steering leaders away from potentially disastrous behaviors, actions, or policies, we rarely see the process or even recognize its results. The media do not typically report preventive actions they do not see or catastrophes that didn't occur.

Similarly, when leaders or organizations self-destruct, we usually see only the visible acts, or failures to act, of the leadership. Unfortunately, courageous followers do not always succeed, despite their best efforts. Attempts that courageous followers may have made to head off the disaster often remain invisible.

As we began the new millennium, contrary to this general rule of courageous follower public invisibility, people around the world got rare glimpses of attempts from below to head off disaster in a range of U.S. institutions. In time, these specific events and personalities will fade from popular view, but leaders would do well to remember such examples as cautionary tales.

In the private sector, headlines were made when a midlevel vice president tried to caution the chairman and CEO of Enron, the country's largest energy trading corporation, that its accounting procedures were egregiously misrepresenting the company's financial position. She took a large personal risk by breaking with the corporate culture and sounding the alarm about these practices. The CEO read the detailed memo prepared by the VP and even interviewed her. Then, instead of treating her information with the utmost seriousness, he referred it to the company's law firm and asked them to investigate the matter but not to make a "detailed analysis" or second-guess the company's outside accountants, effectively quashing the investigation. Shortly thereafter, the company imploded; investors lost virtually everything; thousands of employees lost most of their retirement funds; and the CEO, other former executives, and the midlevel accountants who enabled the fraudulent business practices were indicted and convicted on a range of criminal charges. The chairman/CEO died before being sentenced. His successor, a key architect of the fraud, was sentenced to twenty-four years in prison. Had the CEO only listened to the courageous follower in his ranks and taken her concerns seriously! Perhaps he could have steered the corporate ship, despite the advanced state of its moral rot, to a soft landing instead of a crash and burn.

In the public sector, the new millennium saw the U.S. government and governments around the world reorder their priorities in the wake of the infamous September 11 terrorist attacks on the United States. In the months following these events, information emerged on the attempts by law enforcement field personnel to alert headquarters to specific disturbing signs of impending terrorist activity. Tragically, the systems and culture did not ensure proper attention was given to these warnings. Some of these field personnel subsequently took significant career risks by calling congressional attention to the troubling fact that months later organizational deficiencies, which contributed to the intelligence failures, were still not being adequately remedied.

In the pedophilia scandal that shook the U.S. Catholic Church around the same time as these other events, both the Catholic laity and the general public learned of the numerous attempts to bring the problem to the church hierarchy for remedy. Lay Catholics, individual priests, and Catholic journalists over a period of decades attempted to convey the seriousness of the problem. Instead of meeting these courageous and loyal attempts with courage of their own, the church leadership all too often covered up the problem, allowed abusers to continue wreaking damage on young lives, and stonewalled those raising the issue. In addition to the human suffering this caused, several senior church leaders resigned or were removed, the Catholic Church faced numerous lawsuits resulting in hundreds of millions of dollars of settlement payments, and a number of U.S. dioceses filed for bankruptcy protection. Clearly, the failure of church leaders to value the concerns of loyal followers has wrought great damage on the institution.

These events, and our own experience, confirm that all the courage and skill in the world can't assure that a leader will listen to important feedback. This reality in no way excuses followers from making vigorous efforts to communicate effectively. But it does require an examination of what responsibility leaders have when followers do their best to raise important issues. This is especially so when we, ourselves, are in the leadership role.

In this chapter, we will examine how leaders, intentionally or unintentionally, fail to develop and heed courageous followers, and what they can do to remedy this failure. We will examine this issue from both the perspective of the leader and the perspective of any board or oversight body that shares responsibility for the actions of the organization.

Leaders, by definition, want to succeed. Sometimes their road to success does not lie in the direction they think or cannot be traveled at the speed they believe. By failing to allow for this possibility, despite the signal flags being raised by loyal supporters, many leaders before them have crashed into walls and shattered the dreams of all those who had a stake in the journey. Leaders must learn how and when to listen. If they don't, they may as well cover the instruments on their dashboards, fire their pit crews, and race with abandon down the track, until they destroy their engine or are stopped abruptly by hard external realities.

DO YOU REALLY WANT COURAGEOUS FOLLOWERS?

Almost all leaders say they have an "open door policy" that allows staff to bring troubling matters to their attention. Almost all leaders say they do not want yes men surrounding them. Few sufficiently understand the amount of commitment it takes to realize these desirable states.

Leaders must challenge themselves as to whether they genuinely value acts of courageous followership. Courageous voices often bring difficult news or divergent views. In the moment, they can seem to be an irritant or even thwarting of the leader's ambitions. The challenge for leaders is to see past the immediate discomfort being caused and to value the larger picture of how they and the common purpose are served by the willingness of the follower to raise sensitive issues.

Earlier, we examined the difference between a follower who is highly supportive of a leader and acts as an "Implementer" and a follower who is both highly supportive and willing to challenge a leader's policies or behaviors. We called the latter type a "Partner." Courageous followers are Partners. Leaders need at least a few Partners around them, but Implementers appear to be a leader's dream. They execute the leader's intentions and don't absorb the leader's time with questions or arguments.

It is true that a leader's time is precious. Those who work with a leader need to economize on their use of a leader's time and protect the leader from being stretched too thin. Elevated leaders such as senior executives and officials elected to high office have and need assistants to screen and balance demands on their time. This practice is appropriate.

But leaders can become so pressed for time and so focused on implementation of their agenda that they find it difficult to listen patiently to followers, even if they are direct reports, who want to take time to raise an important concern. These leaders may technically have an open door policy but treat those who walk through it in ways that severely limit their ability to convey their concerns and their willingness to raise future concerns. As a result, such leaders rarely hear divergent views and interpret the absence of these as agreement with their ideas and support for their policies. This may be so. But it is also an indication that there are potentially serious blind spots in these leaders' appreciation of critical events and the likely impact of decisions being made in response to these events.

Because leaders' direct reports usually have some access to them, and hopefully some latitude to offer divergent views, it is perhaps even more important to establish this potential with staff who don't report directly to the leader. Disciplined leaders practice some version of management by walking around to keep a finger on the pulse of things. Depending on the size and spatial configuration of the organization, they find ways to do this both physically and virtually. But doing this does not ensure they will hear about sensitive issues. That, of course, is the function of the open door policy. However, the dynamics of an open door policy are more complex than is usually realized.

It is rare for employees to request a meeting with a senior executive who is two or three levels above them, unless they are tasked to report on an issue. It is rare to bypass the next level in the chain of command to raise a sensitive issue at a higher level because of the potential for damaging the relationships with the people who have the most direct power to punish or reward them. A leader who receives bad news or a request from two or three levels down the command chain to meet must treat it seriously. Those who guard the leader's time can be authorized to gather information about the nature of the requested meeting, but they should not be authorized to block it without informing the leader.

Leaders of large organizations often cannot imagine what they don't know about their organizations. They typically have prescribed information channels that filter information before it reaches them. If junior members of an organization overcome the psychological and cultural inhibitions against jumping levels in the chain of command, there is a reasonable chance that the information they want to give the leader is important. With the exception of requests to meet about individual personnel matters, which we will deal with later in this chapter, it is almost always advisable for the leader to meet with the staff member.

What leaders do in and after that meeting, however, will determine whether this or any other employee risks bringing sensitive information to them in the future. How do they receive the employee's information? Do they listen well, or do they interrupt and intimidate the employee? Do they do anything meaningful to act on and follow up on the issue? Do they do so in a way that does not come back to haunt the employee? Do they ask further questions about how they themselves may be contributing to the problem? Do they seek the employee's ideas on other questions that may affect the organization? Whether the employee experiences the contact with the leader as good or painful, useful or not, word will fly around either way and ingrain itself in the fabric of the culture.

 As a leader, do not mistake the fact that you say you have an open door policy for having one that functions. The acid test is whether staff actually come to you with tough issues about corporate behavior or your own behavior or policies.

If you rarely receive requests from staff to use the open door policy, it usually means that factors are inhibiting its use that outweigh the perceived benefits of taking advantage of it. If you understand the value of fostering courageous followership, you need to examine what those factors might be. How can you do this?

Keep a standing open door meeting time on your calendar, and promote the fact. If it doesn't get used much, investigate why.

Ask individual staff whether you do anything that dissuades them from using the open door policy; press for a substantive answer.

Ask senior staff who report to you to pose this question for you; they may get answers that you would not hear directly.

When these staff report their findings, thank them and avoid the impulse to defend yourself.

Check your understanding of what they are telling you by asking whether you displayed any of the dissuading behaviors in this particular meeting.

If you did display that behavior, make sure you understand exactly what it consisted of: tone of voice, body language, choice of verbal language, and so on.

For example, some leaders pride themselves on not suffering fools gladly. This may be one of the characteristics that enabled them to reach the heights of leadership. But this very characteristic, which cuts through excuses or long-winded explanations, can also block critical information from reaching the leader. Tempering a tendency to impatiently challenge a point being developed by a nervous employee can open channels that are otherwise unavailable to high-powered executives. An open door policy is only effective in proportion to the leader's listening skills. Leaders who get feedback that they are weak in this area are well advised to make improving their listening skills a high priority.

WHAT MESSAGES ARE NUMBER TWOS SENDING?

As a leader, you are not the only one who sets the tone in the organization. Those closest to you may have considerably more operational contact with staff and, therefore, as much or more influence on corporate culture. Because of this, they may, intentionally or not, create an atmosphere that inhibits staff from sending you important information. This can work in many ways:

> In their efforts to support you and help you manage your time, they may be overprotective.

> You may have implicitly given them the unofficial role of "bad cops" who are to keep complaints from reaching you.

> They may find information someone wants to give you personally threatening or threatening to a colleague they consider an ally.

> They may be perceived to be so close to you that your loyalty to them won't allow you to hear complaints about their behavior.

> The qualities that suit them for their functional roles may not suit them for being your intermediary.

> As a leader, you are responsible not only for the cultural and moral tone you set personally, but also for the tone set by those with whom you surround yourself.

You must stay alert to this tone. Regardless of how or why the flow of important information gets interrupted, it can be detrimental to your decision making. If you have shone the light on yourself and corrected any ways in which you personally have dissuaded staff from communicating critical information, yet you still rarely hear divergent or troublesome views, you need to look further. What message are staff getting from other members of your direct team who are perceived to wield power in the organization?

You might go about this as follows:

Ask staff, informally or by confidential survey, if they are being dissuaded from appropriately using the open door policy to communicate with you.

If you discover staff are being dissuaded from using the open door policy, clearly reiterate your values and expectations in this regard to your direct reports.

Do not do so accusatorily because this may generate trouble for the junior staff. If you get a whiff of subsequent retaliatory action against staff who bring information to you, take disciplinary action that sends an unequivocal message across the organization.

Ask your senior staff whether you seem to be conveying conflicting values to them regarding communication to you. If so, clarify your intention and the procedures to use.

Your team will tend to act in ways they believe you value. Pay attention to their behavior and use it as a mirror for the values you are projecting.

APPRECIATING AND ACCEPTING SUPPORT

Leaders usually have an extremely high work ethic. They often think nothing of working sixty- or seventy-hour weeks or more. This is especially so for leaders whose organizations are start-ups, are in crisis, or have complex constituencies with demanding customers, intense social missions, or multisite locations requiring significant travel.

In addition to the very real external demands on their time, some leaders exacerbate the situation by involving themselves in the details of decision making, communications, or other matters that would be better handled at a lower level.

Whatever the cause, when leaders work excessive hours, it is rarely a cost-neutral phenomenon. Sooner or later, doing so takes a toll. The toll can take many forms. Organizationally, leaders may become bottlenecks, the quality of their decision making may suffer, or they may become bad tempered, hurting the morale of those with whom they are unfairly gruff. Sometimes the toll is on their personal lives, though it may not be evident until they are involved in a divorce or become run-down and ill.

The staff members who work most closely with a leader can see this pattern developing early. Often, they try to step in to relieve the leader of some pressure. Leaders don't always accept these offers of help well. Corporate cultures tend to reward leaders showing toughness, not vulnerability. As a result, they sometimes let themselves get stretched too far before asking for or accepting help.

There is a gray area between trying to support leaders by relieving them of certain pressures and challenging leaders who are insufficiently aware of the effect their work schedule and habits are having on the organization.

Sometimes leaders stay too involved in one aspect of their duties because they are particularly strong in those areas or like them. Sometimes they do not trust others to perform the job to their standards. They mistake their role as being responsible for the work of the organization, whereas the more important role for a leader is building a highly competent team that is responsible for the work of the organization. Sometimes they do not realize how driven they are. Sometimes they are simply disorganized.

Leaders must be very alert to offers by staff to unburden them of duties or to help them perform those duties. They should not lightly dismiss these offers; rather, they should be curious as to why staff are making the offers. Questions they might ask both the staff and themselves include the following:

> "Do you think I am overly involved in this particular activity? If so, in what ways?"

> "What effect is my involvement having on the staff and on the process?"

> "Who else could perform this function, and what would they need to do to meet the standards I have for it?"

> "Am I not paying sufficient attention to other needs of the organization? If so, what are these?"

"How much is the strain I'm under showing, and what other changes do you think I should consider making?"

Leaders can take advantage of the staff's concerns to achieve better work-life balance for themselves and to deploy their own energies more strategically. In addition, this situation presents an excellent opportunity to demonstrate to staff that they can influence their leaders. This experience is useful in creating a culture that supports and develops courageous followership.

APPRECIATING CONSTRUCTIVE CHALLENGE MORE

It is not difficult to conceive of appreciating followers who find new ways to support their leaders. It takes a greater stretch of the imagination to conceive of appreciating staff who challenge the way in which you are leading.

Imagine for a moment that you as a leader are surrounded with people who deeply appreciate your vision, your integrity, your communication and organization skills, your strategic and tactical thinking, and your ability to get people to commit to the mission of the organization. This sounds pretty good.

Now imagine for a moment that they admire you so much that they will not tell you anything negative, including these points:

> You have misspelled the name of your most important client or contributor in a letter that is about to be mailed.

> You are unknowingly violating a key cultural norm of an international VIP you are hosting.

> You are about to sign off on the financial statement of the company when they know there is a serious flaw in it that could land you in legal trouble.

Any of these examples sound ludicrous, and irresponsible on the part of the people surrounding you. Of course, you want to be corrected in these matters! You don't pretend to be perfect. You expect your staff to keep you from making errors!

But what about the following examples? If you were the head of an organization or department, would you really want staff to tell you what they are thinking in the following instances?

> **You are so forceful and intellectually intimidating at meetings that no one wants to risk embarrassment by raising questions or alternate ideas for consideration.**
>
> **You are losing the trust of key staff and board members because you seem more interested in your compensation package than in the welfare of the organization.**
>
> **You are pushing through more mergers and acquisitions than the organization can assimilate productively, and this action is endangering the company's viability.**

The first set of examples would clearly save you from embarrassment, or worse. The second set hits more of a nerve. They challenge some aspect of your values, style, or vision. It would take a lot more for you to appreciate being confronted in this manner. Needless to say, it would also take a lot more for staff to get up the courage to challenge you in this way.

Yet, from an organizational point of view, it is at least as important that you be told the second set of observations as the first. These perceptions are likely to have more long-term impact on your career and the organization's success. How do you make sure that you create a climate in which you hear *and pay attention to* feedback of this nature that you might rather not hear?

The first thing you must do is to examine your own beliefs about authority and what is appropriate to say to those in authority and what is not. You may have had role models, either when growing up or working early in your career, who did not tolerate questioning or disagreement and viewed it as insubordination. If so, you would do well to ferret out these models, examine them, and reclassify them as poor examples of contemporary leadership style. Contemporary financial, legal, technical, social, political, and communication systems are so complex that you cannot be the "authority" in all areas.

Next, reflect on your comfort with criticism. It is very natural to react to criticism defensively. You undoubtedly have observed your peers or subordinates do this many times when you have tried to bring a problem or situation to their attention. There was no need for them to respond defensively, as you were not blaming or attacking them but simply bringing something to their attention that needed remedy. Yet, they became defensive.

Now imagine if you respond in this quite normal human way to a subordinate who has the courage to raise a sensitive matter with you. Because of the position of formal authority and power that you occupy, if you react defensively, you are unlikely to hear further about this matter or be given any other feedback that individual may have for you. Therefore, we can conclude the following:

 A requisite of good leadership is to override naturally defensive feelings, statements, and behaviors and display genuine interest in what sources of critical feedback are telling you.

This is so central to developing world-class leadership and followership that it bears repeating. It is that crucial.

A requisite of good leadership is to override naturally defensive feelings, statements, and behaviors and display genuine interest in what sources of critical feedback are telling you.

The need to develop this capacity is often unrecognized or given insufficient importance. It is not easy to do. Initially, it may require considerable self-discipline, but, with practice, even those who find this posture uncomfortable can come to appreciate giving and receiving feedback.

Finally, you have to demonstrate responsiveness to feedback. There is no point in staff taking risks to give you critical feedback on sensitive issues if they never see a return on the risk. You may or may not accept or act on the feedback, but you need to demonstrate that you are responsive to it. Here are a number of different levels of response as examples:

"I've thought about what you said the other day, and I'm not going to act on it for the following reasons. . . . But I appreciate your bringing the matter to my attention, and I hope you'll do so again if it still seems to be a problem."

"I was pretty skeptical about what you said the other day, but, on reflection, I realized that you might be right, so I'm giving it further consideration."

"I've thought about what you said, and here are the actions I've taken. . . . I know it's not everything you thought I should do, but I want you to know that I took what you said seriously."

"I heard what you said the other day, and I'm going to try to make the changes you suggested. I probably won't do it perfectly, but I want you to know I'm working on it."

"I realize the seriousness of the discussion we had the other day, and I've taken five major steps to address the issue. Please give them a few weeks to take effect, and then let me know whether you start to see changes or not."

A few leaders are naturally good about creating a relaxed atmosphere in which staff can give them critical feedback. Most have to make a conscious effort to create such an environment. Few acts are more essential to the long-term success of leaders and their organizations.

INVITING CREATIVE CHALLENGE

Although feedback is a critical component of the leader-follower system, it is reactive. Beyond feedback there is a proactive mode of operating in which ideas are continuously sought, encouraged, developed, examined, challenged, modified, synthesized, and adopted or discarded.

A creative culture emerges when there is a commitment to broadening participation and seeking diverse perspectives, to challenging the status quo and the obvious solution. When a group relishes this spirit of creative challenge, it rolls back its limits and finds new ways of pursuing its purpose.

It is critical that leaders distinguish between challenge to their authority and challenge to their ideas. This clear distinction permits an environment of open dialogue and vibrant creativity. Confusion in this arena is stifling.

Even leaders who philosophically welcome creative challenge need to understand how they might inadvertently discourage it:

Leaders often grasp situations and opportunities with great internal speed and want to rapidly implement the ideas they formulate in response to these.

Leaders are prone to communicating their ideas with great energy and conviction, which is part of their gift.

When leaders present their own ideas for action before giving their team a chance to generate a range of options, they inhibit further dialogue.

A leader's premature display of conviction about an idea discourages creative challenge, as a would-be challenger does not want to appear negative or disloyal.

Too often, a CEO spends a whole meeting presenting a "great new idea" more or less as a fait accompli, and then asks whether it poses any problems. The people around the table know he's made up his mind and doesn't really want to hear about problems or concerns. So they don't speak up. There is no process that invites creative dialogue.

To make full use of the team's intellectual resources, leaders need to formally or informally establish norms of behavior that encourage creative challenge. These might include the following:

Information about situations of major import to the group is broadly shared so it can be factored into the thinking of all team members.

Dialogue is invited about important decisions that will impact the group.

To encourage uninhibited thinking, processes are established for generating creative approaches that are distinct from the processes for evaluating those approaches.

Distinctions are made between an idea and its originator so status does not cloud value; as appropriate, methods for anonymously presenting ideas are used.

Group members, including the leader, improve their communication and meeting skills so they don't discourage contributors through words, voice tone, or body language.

Sacred cows are gently led to pasture—all relevant options are open for discussion.

Even "wild" ideas are not discounted but examined for what new ways of thinking they may open.

Even "sensible" ideas are tested against different scenarios to see whether they hold up under scrutiny.

Once leaders demonstrate commitment to a participatory process, the behavior of individuals in the group often changes perceptibly in ways that enhance group interaction. If leaders regress to an earlier, less participatory mode, followers can hold the leader accountable to the norms of creative dialogue that have been established. True partnerships can be founded in this climate, and exceptional teamwork can emerge.

A CULTURE OF COMMUNICATION, NOT COMPLAINTS

Inviting creative challenge is a high level of innovative teamwork. It can be undermined by the lack of a more basic set of group norms governing interpersonal relationships.

Too often leadership teams are plagued with internal fractiousness. There is mistrust or misunderstanding laterally among members of the team as well as a degree of upward resentment. The fracture lines might run along gender or ethnic divisions, between functions or regions, between staff who came from different organizational cultures that were merged, between older and newer staff, or between staff with very different personalities or agendas. Whatever its source, members of the team develop the dysfunctional habit of complaining to each other or the senior leader about fellow team members. They fail to take up the complaint with the person or persons who need to be addressed in order to resolve it: those who are the target of their complaints.

When leaders observe this behavior, they can be sure it is a sign that there are also complaints about themselves that they are not hearing. Complaining has become acceptable in the culture. It has become the substitute for courageous, honest, and productive dialogue. In fact, leaders themselves may be engaging in this behavior, complaining to senior staff about each other and thus setting the tone for this behavior.

When team members bring complaints about each other to the leader, a mistake that leaders make is listening to the complaints and thereby colluding with the dysfunctional culture. In most cases it is preferable for a leader to say something like this:

> "This sounds important. Let's get _____ [the target of the complaint] in here and straighten this out."

If possible, get the other party in there right then and present the issue as a matter of perceptions, not facts. This is a no-fault process. It takes the complaint, which is an interpretation of the other's intention and behavior and sometimes an assessment of the other's competence, and attempts to break it down into an information exchange about what actually occurred and why those actions were taken. Often, the grounds for the complaint disappear once all the information is available to both parties. If not, sufficient information emerges to allow the situation to become a learning experience for one or both parties, or to clarify further steps that are needed to resolve it. The leader might ask a question of the two parties along these lines:

> "_____ [the one making the complaint] is concerned that you appear to have done _____ . Could you fill us in on the situation and what you did so we can understand it better?"

More important than clarifying the particular situation, you are modeling the value of directly addressing issues with each other and thereby strengthening the team. By making direct communication the expected action, you are supporting a culture of courageous relationships. This behavior inevitably will extend to team members' relationships with you.

The leadership task is to build a culture in which conflict is handled through healthy and creative dialogue. Leaders have enormous influence in this regard. If they don't handle conflict well themselves or if they allow it to stay below the surface, significant damage can be done to the ability of the leadership team to perform its function effectively. If leaders handle this scenario well, they can have a high degree of confidence that they, too, are hearing what they need to hear about themselves, instead of everyone but them hearing it.

CREATING PROTECTED COMMUNICATION CHANNELS

While in an ideal world all members of your organization would behave as courageous followers, it is no more realistic to expect perfection from followers than for them to expect perfection of their leaders.

A follower may not bring sensitive information or divergent perspectives to a leader's attention for a number of reasons:

Perceived earlier instances of retaliation by the leader

Perceived earlier instances of retaliation by those with whom the leader may discuss issues

Uncertainty about or incompleteness of information

Disbelief that remedies will be taken to make the risk of speaking up worthwhile

Personal stresses (family health insurance needs, etc.) that make the risks of speaking up seem too high.

It is useful to provide the staff in your organization with a low-risk way of raising issues that are of concern to them. A classic method is to appoint an ombudsman. If you endow this position with the right power and policies, it can save you and the organization endless grief.

Creating an ombudsman role may seem counter to the spirit of building a culture of courageous relationships in which staff address problems they have with those most directly concerned. But this role can be performed in ways that support such a culture. Speaking confidentially with the ombudsman to air thoughts, have a sounding board, and seek advice is far removed from complaining unproductively to those who have no power to help remedy a situation. And, for some, it still represents an act of courage to speak frankly to the ombudsman despite assurances of confidentiality.

Appointing an ombudsman also helps protect leaders from a form of pressure that can be unhealthy for the organization. Often, staff will use an ombudsman to air grievances over compensation and benefits issues and seek advice for formally redressing these if appropriate. In the absence of an ombudsman, frustrated staff will eventually take the matter to the CEO or vice president level. This puts senior executives in the awkward position of using their power to remedy individual staff problems. Word gets around when this happens, and it inadvertently creates a process of taking individual problems to them. For numerous reasons, this approach is not the best use of a leader's energy. It also creates potential problems of perceived favoritism, rancor if the problem is not solved to staff members' satisfaction, and other issues.

Certain conditions must be met if the ombudsman position is to function well. It is as dangerous to have a nonfunctioning ombudsman as it is to have a nonfunctioning safety valve. The professional societies that represent ombudsmen publish best practice guidelines. Respecting these guidelines, adequate attention must be given to the following success factors:

Select an individual who

enjoys or can generate widespread trust among staff;

has deep organizational knowledge and can put issues into a sophisticated context for both staff and the general public;

has the skills needed to coach employees to solve their own problems when this is appropriate, thereby supporting a culture of courageous relationships.

Ensure that

the ombudsman has the resources to perform the role with privacy;

the ombudsman has the open door access needed to resolve issues when given the consent by the individual bringing the issue to raise it with others;

the ombudsman has the responsibility and immunity to keep walking through that door until a particular issue is resolved;

processes exist for the tracking and timely resolution of issues brought to the ombudsman.

Make it a rule to

never, never casually discuss with others a sensitive personnel issue brought to you by the ombudsman or allow other executives to do so—treat each such conversation as a trust;

meet periodically with the ombudsman to discuss patterns of issues that could escalate to become major ethical, legal, operational, or public relations matters;

use the full range of communication vehicles to reinforce the value of courageous relationships and the availability of the ombudsman to help resolve issues.

Your aim is to ensure that critical information about the behavior and operations of the organization and its managers reaches whatever level is necessary to address these matters effectively. Courageous followers are responsible for conveying that information despite personal risk. Leaders are responsible for creating the institutional atmosphere and channels that lower these risks. Make sure these channels exist, and periodically confirm that they are clear of bureaucratic or cultural blockages.

DISCERNMENT: WHAT IS THE RIGHT ACTION?

It is self-evident that leaders who have multiple channels providing them with feedback on the impact of their policies, programs, management style, and processes are in the best position to effect continuous correction, improvement, and growth. The channels can consist of a mix of formal and informal reporting processes, internal and external auditors, task forces and consulting teams, open door policies and ombudsmen, and other vehicles within the constraints of an organization's resources.

When these channels provide clear and consistent feedback, there is a strong chance that the information is both valid and important. Course corrections or even transformation may be needed. Leaders ignore this information at their peril even, or especially, if it flies in the face of their cherished beliefs. At other times, the feedback is inconsistent and represents a range of divergent views that do not necessarily invalidate the leadership's core strategy and methods of operation but do throw them into question. How should a leader respond to these discordant streams of information?

The very act of leadership often puts leaders out in front of their organizations or constituents. Acting only on the input or feedback of followers or peers would negate the act of leadership itself. Yet it is dangerous to simply ignore these voices when they strongly diverge from a leader's perceptions or each other's. Further analytical tools can be brought to bear on the issues, but even these do not necessarily provide conclusive evidence of the right course of action. In the face of this scenario, leaders are left at the core juncture of the leader's role: *which way to go?* At this juncture, there is a great temptation for leaders to stick with their beliefs, to "go with their gut" and to "hang tough." If they prove to be right, they are heroes. If they prove to be wrong, the organization and its people can pay a heavy price. How do leaders make sure they are striking the right balance between following their internal guiding lights and listening to the concerned voices of courageous followers?

At such points, leaders need to shift gears and make concerted efforts to sort out which beliefs and actions are well grounded and which may be misguided. This process can be described as *discernment*. Quakers use this term for the process of distinguishing what is a "true calling" and what is ego-driven activity. Although, in contrast to Quakers, we are not necessarily invoking a spiritual dimension, it is useful to make the distinction between purpose-driven and ego-driven acts. Is a policy, strategy, or set of behaviors truly serving the common purpose, or has a leader or leadership team become so invested in it that pursuing it is now primarily serving other needs? For example, the need to remain in charge, to be right, to feel important and powerful, to be successful and handsomely compensated, or to protect themselves? While these possible motivations are rarely if ever admitted, too often they play a disproportionate role in ill-advised leadership actions.

It is far more preferable for leaders to sort out their motivations themselves before events overtake them and force the issue. If transformation is needed, leaders who resist change until their backs are to the wall, and only then frantically act to save their positions and/or organizations, are harshly judged as having done too little, too late. The desire to retain the status quo when it confers on us power, prestige, and rewards is understandably strong. It acts as a powerful filter that cancels out the gravity or urgency that others see in a situation. But timing in leadership is hugely important. We rarely get second chances on the big issues.

The process of discernment requires a deep level of examination. The process is more than one of just weighing options. It is a soul-searching attempt to distinguish between what course is driven by self-interest, pride, or attachment to a particular strategy, project, or individual and what course is driven by an overriding service to the common purpose.

The difficulty of discerning our true motives should not be underestimated. We want to believe that we are good people. To support this belief, we are prone to constructing persuasive rationalizations that allow us to feel comfortable with our decisions and actions. Significant issues may also be at stake regarding our reputation, security, or financial compensation. It is often advisable to seek the help of others in this process. It may be a trusted adviser or a cross section of trusted advisers. Leaders or leadership teams who seek help must have confidence in the confidentiality of the process to allow them to be fully honest.

Discernment requires asking ourselves or allowing others whom we trust to ask us questions such as these:

> **What hierarchy of values should be governing this decision? What core conflicts in values are occurring?**
>
> **What would a picture of success look like if the common purpose were well served in this matter?**

Will taking a course of action to which the leader is inclined pose any undue risks to the common purpose?

What habits, self-interest, or ego-driven factors exist that may be competing with the best interests of the common purpose?

Are any perspectives, information, or ethical issues being devalued because they conflict with these factors?

Is the leader's inclination or behavior in this matter a specific instance of a larger pattern that should be examined?

In the final analysis, leaders must act. They must do so when they do not have all the information they would like, when their motives are mixed, and when they cannot be fully certain that what they are doing will best serve the organization. The process of reflection and consultation cannot be allowed to lead to paralysis. Decisions always carry risk. But leaders have the responsibility to know themselves, as well as their organizations, and always to act with the best interests of the common purpose in mind. This responsibility does not mean that their own legitimate interests cannot be served, but it does mean that, consciously or unconsciously, these must not take dominance over the common good. This is a high standard to live up to, and groups are fortunate to have leaders who meet it and followers who help them do so.

THE ROLE OF THE BOARD

Most organizations have a board of directors or its equivalent. This body is charged with ensuring that the leadership of an organization is performing successfully and acting within the generally accepted practices or rules governing its type of activity. Because the board is responsible for the integrity and effectiveness of the organization's leadership, it is in its interest to share responsibility for creating the conditions that foster courageous followership. How can the board do so without encroaching on the role of the CEO?

Leader-follower roles are complex at board level. Well-run boards provide conceptual leadership for the organization by setting the broad policies that guide its focus and define expected standards of ethical behavior. CEOs must follow the board's collective leadership in this regard and they are accountable to the board. At the same time, boards rely on the CEO to provide vision and tangible leadership to the organization. They often perform exhaustive searches to find the right individual to do this. It would be self-defeating if they did not then follow the CEO's lead.

The board has clear fiduciary responsibility to ensure the organization is successfully pursuing its mission with sound policies. In a legal sense, the board must assert its right to ensure the CEO is following the mandate given by the board. In a practical sense, it often operates in relation to the CEO from the "Partner" quadrant of the Courageous Follower model, both supporting and challenging the CEO as appropriate.

The current corporate practice in the United States of investing the role of board chair and CEO in the same individual further complicates leadership and followership roles at board level. But even where this model is not followed or has been supplanted by dividing these roles, the relationships are complex.

To make this complex set of relationships work so the board effectively performs its functions and does not become a rubber stamp, boards need to set policies that establish adequate information channels to them. They cannot solely depend on information massaged and packaged by the CEO's office. But neither can they undermine the CEO through off-channel communications or, worse, micromanage the CEO. How can boards manage the tension in this set of dynamics?

We once again return to the primary model of this book. Leaders and followers, including CEOs and board members, serve the common purpose. If this organizing principle is kept in focus, efforts to serve it effectively are less likely to be construed as lack of personal trust in each other.

The board needs to develop clear policies setting mission-based performance expectations and values-based standards that set the permissible boundaries of staff behavior while they work to meet these expectations. Then it needs to develop a diverse set of internal and external reporting mechanisms that allow it to monitor adherence to these policies. Many models that a board can use for carrying out its tasks are available.

In relationship to supporting a culture of courageous followership, the board should explicitly consider how to deal with the following issues:

> **Under what circumstances will it expect the ombudsman or the internal auditor to bring a matter directly to the attention of the board?**
>
> **How will it handle unsolicited communication from other staff to the board in order to protect staff's willingness to bring issues to its attention when appropriate?**
>
> **What norms of behavior will be established that allow individual executives to bring matters to the board's attention without it seeming disloyal to the CEO?**

These issues are fraught with sensitivities that can harm the amicable relationships of boards and senior executive teams. But they must be dealt with openly and maturely. Recent legislation in the United States mandates some of these reporting mechanisms and protections for staff, but ultimately it depends on the courage and skill of board members to bring these policies to life.

If boards do not stand behind executives and staff who bring what they consider to be serious matters to the board's attention, they will cut off the flow of potentially critical information. They must insist that the CEO and other executives place loyalty to the organization first. When staff act out of organizational loyalty, they must not allow individual executives to treat this as personal disloyalty. Fail to do this, and the board will find staff going to regulators, lawyers, and the press, instead of to them, to seek redress for matters the board could and should resolve.

Experienced board members and executives both know that disaffected staff can abuse such channels of communication. Each must have confidence in the other's judgment to distinguish between vindictive or unbalanced reporting and matters of genuine concern. Likewise, each must understand the importance of having multiple channels on which information can flow that reveals the need for organizational correction so those with the information do not have to seek channels outside the organization. In the long run, this serves everyone's interest.

At the same time, the board needs to avoid creating a role for itself that inadvertently undermines a culture of courageous relationships between the CEO and staff. A CEO should be charged with the responsibility for creating an environment in which staff feel secure in bringing matters that threaten the common purpose to the attention of the people in the organization who can remedy them. If the board finds staff coming to it with any frequency, instead of to the executives responsible, it can task one or more of its members to mentor the CEO and other executives. If this approach does not produce the desired result, it can task the CEO to identify and implement a developmental program that will build the awareness and skills to create a healthy, self-correcting organizational culture that serves the common purpose well.

A board that ignores signs that the organization culture needs to better support courageous followership is setting the stage for principled staff to be forced to go outside the organization for remedy. If this is the case, a board will have failed in its responsibility as stewards of the organization.

RESPONDING TO A MORAL STAND

A defining moment for leadership occurs when it is confronted with a moral stand by a follower. What leadership does next may affect the fate of the organization and its leaders for years to come.

If followers feel the need to take a moral stand, leadership has already missed or closed itself off to many earlier signals. This may be its last chance to pay attention. But it is a great challenge to listen to the criticism implicit in a moral stand. If the stand taken is directly related to your actions as leader, it will, naturally, trigger impulses of self-defense or self-preservation. If the moral stand brings to your attention serious charges against other levels of leadership, it may produce a reaction of shock, denial, or conflicted loyalties.

A common response is to devalue the individuals taking the stand. It is the easiest and also the worst possible response. One can always find flaws in individuals, the case they are making, or their methods. These must be put into the context of the fact that individuals taking a courageous stand are risking a lot and are unlikely to be taking the stand gratuitously. Seeking to understand what *is* valid about their concerns, rather than focusing on what is *not* valid, must come first.

Another common response is to devalue the charges. They may seem implausible, exaggerated, or even hysterical and outrageous. This may be so. But it is the unthinkable that can sometimes go unnoticed and do terrible damage to an organization by the time it eventually comes to attention. Do not dismiss charges that seem outlandish until you have conducted a careful, not cursory, investigation. And do not devalue charges that may seem plausible but relatively unimportant to you. They are clearly important to someone else who just may be a better weather vane of public sentiment than you.

The moral stand may take the range of forms we have examined, including refusing to cooperate in an activity, bringing a situation to the attention of a higher level within the organization, and threatening to publicly resign if a situation is not remedied. Just as it is useful to have procedures in place for responding to potential crises, it is useful to have a procedure for responding to a moral confrontation to the organization or its individual officers. Here is a possible response protocol:

Separate the message from the messenger. Pay careful attention to the content regardless of your view of the messenger.

Listen both to the content and to the strength of feelings about the matter. The seriousness of the situation is better gauged by both factors.

Regardless of your initial reaction, promise to get back to the individual personally, and commit to a time frame for doing so.

Avoid any impulse to take precipitous and poorly advised damage control measures, such as document destruction.

Decide which advisers to consult, bearing in mind as necessary which relationships confer legal protections for privileged communications.

With the help of your advisers, gather any additional information you need to understand the full scope of the situation.

With this additional information, play out the potential consequences, including worst-case scenarios, avoiding any tendency to denial.

Review and restate the core values that will guide your course of action. Generate two or three options for consideration that respect these values, and respond sufficiently to the gravity of the situation.

Choose the course of action that best serves the common purpose, and act with the vigor, courage, and imagination the situation warrants.

Report back personally to the individual or individuals whose moral stand provided the catalyst for your actions.

As the situation progresses, credit the courageous followers who took the moral stand, while accepting responsibility personally or corporately for the wrong actions now being corrected.

Such a protocol may be executed in as little as several hours or as long as several weeks. Time is not generally on your side in these situations, and speed can be as important as proper deliberation. The crucial act of leadership is to respond to a moral stand in an equally principled manner—and meet courage with courage.

GROWTH AS BOTH LEADER AND FOLLOWER

Human beings give meaning to their lives through constellations of commitments. The commitments they make span the range from personal development, to family, to groups and organizations, to vocations and avocations, to local or global causes, to perceived spiritual truths.

Some of these commitments are solitary pursuits for knowledge or pleasure, but most are inextricably social in nature. As soon as we enter the social arena, we are involved with leadership and followership roles. The less rigidly that our culture or an activity prescribes these relationships, the more fluid they may be; in some situations we lead, in others we follow, and in still others we move back and forth between these roles or share them equally with our fellows.

As we make our unique journeys through life, we have ample opportunities to grow in these roles. Sometimes we succeed in our roles, and sometimes we fail. We must be careful to learn from both these experiences and also careful not to learn too well from either. Success leads us to rely too heavily on what has worked for us in the past, and failure leads us to rely too heavily on others whose ends appear successful but whose means may be questionable.

Growth in both the leader and follower roles requires consciousness of how we perform them now and how we might perform them better in the future. Growth requires motivation, especially our own internal motivation, and a commitment to the hard work needed to change comfortable behaviors and develop well-honed skills. Finally, growth requires feedback loops from others to help us gauge how we are doing and how much more there may be to do.

As a leader and a follower—for yes, you are both—use the laboratory of your relationships to generate the necessary conditions for growth. As a follower, do not place too much blame on leaders for what is wrong; and as a leader, do not place too much blame on followers. Each has the capacity to influence and improve the other. Work to develop the courage and skill to use this capacity effectively.

When we improve in our roles as leader and follower, the common purposes to which we have committed ourselves benefit. This is the meaningful legacy we leave in the wake of our life trajectory.

EPILOGUE

THE WHOLESOME USE OF POWER does not assure success in achieving objectives, but it is in itself success.

Both the common purpose and our integrity are served when core values guide us. The exercise of power presumes the hope for success and the willingness to risk failure, but a values centered use of power assures that even if goal achievement failures occur, they will not be compounded by failures of human decency.

The rewards of the balanced leader-follower relationship are the rewards of all healthy relationships—honest struggle, growth, mutual admiration, and even love. A reward of the wholesome use of power is the opportunity to witness improvements in the lives of those we serve. When leaders and followers fulfill their respective roles, they give each other the gift of being able to serve well. This service adds meaning to our lives.

Courage is a prerequisite to healthy relationships and a fulfilling life. Courageous leaders and followers working together sow seeds. When circumstances do not let them reap the harvest themselves, they leave the soil enriched by their integrity and commitment for the next planting.

MEDITATION ON FOLLOWERSHIP

FOR ME, BECOMING A COURAGEOUS FOLLOWER, like becoming a good human being, is both a daily and a lifelong task. Visualizing a desired state helps to realize it. I share this meditation as one visualization of the state I aspire to. You may want to refer to it from time to time.

I am a steward of this group and share responsibility for its success.

I am responsible for adhering to the highest values I can envision.

I am responsible for my successes and failures and for continuing to learn from them.

I am responsible for the attractive and unattractive parts of who I am.

I can empathize with others who are also imperfect.

As an adult, I can relate on a peer basis to other adults who are the group's formal leaders.

I can support leaders and counsel them, and receive support and counsel from them.

Our common purpose is our best guide.

I have the power to help leaders use their power wisely and effectively.

If leaders abuse power, I can help them change their behavior.

If I abuse power, I can learn from others and change my behavior.

If abusive leaders do not change their behavior, I can and will withdraw my support.

By staying true to my values, I can serve others well and fulfill my potential.

Thousands of courageous acts by followers can, one by one, improve the world.

Courage always exists in the present. What can I do today?

ACKNOWLEDGMENTS

I SHOWED THE FIRST THIN DRAFT OF THIS BOOK to my friend
Steven Bosacker, an astute management thinker and, at the time, a chief
of staff to a member of the U.S. Congress. His early encouragement of the
work was crucial to my continuing the project. Other early readers who
gave both encouragement and much-needed criticism include Dr. Janet
Poley, U.S. representative Tim Penny, Dr. Jeff Fishel, Dr. Susan Hammond,
Frank Gregorsky, Diane Thompson, Sara King, Kirk Stromberg, and Olivia
Mellan.

Readers of later drafts provided equally crucial encouragement and
feedback: Duncan Campbell, Bill Schmidt, Dr. Jack J. Phillips, Jim Liebig,
Major Don Zacherl, Laura Scott, Helen Foster, Frank Basler, Gordon
MacKenzie, Prudence Goforth, General Walter Ulmer, and my friend who
has seen me through good times and bad times as a leader and follower,
Ron Hopkins. I am particularly thankful to Jim Liebig for challenging a
key weakness in the manuscript so that I could correct it, and to Bill
Schmidt for urging me to emphasize "the common purpose" as the center
of the leader-follower relationship.

Primary thanks for timely and substantive help on the second edition goes to Gene Dixon, who, has since completed his dissertation on followership and has become a mentor to other scholars working in the field. I am particularly indebted to Gene for suggesting that my original model of courageous followership would be enhanced by expanding "The Courage to Leave" into "The Courage to Take Moral Action." I also wish to thank him and others who provided peer review of the chapter "The Courage to Listen to Followers," including Brent Uken, who has championed courageous followership throughout his career at Ernst & Young LLP.

In addition to some of the above stalwarts who also reviewed "The Courage to Speak to the Hierarchy," I owe thanks for supportive critiques of this newest chapter to Don Jacobson of the U.S. Foreign Service; Gail Williams of NASA's Goddard Space Flight Center; Don Noack of Sandia National Laboratories; my colleagues Don Frazer, Ralph Bates, Elisabeth Higgins Null, and Jay Hurwitz; and my fellow Berrett-Koehler author, Pat McLagan.

I will reiterate in this edition my thanks for the years of support and encouragement I have received in a variety of ways from my colleagues at the Institute for Business Technology, the Congressional Management Foundation, and Executive Coaching & Consulting Associates who display so many of the attributes of courageous followership.

To this list I will add my appreciation for Dr. Jean Lipman-Blumen and Dr. Ron Riggio, who both have distinguished careers at Claremont University and currently serve on the board of the International Leadership Association (ILA). Their support for the first national conference on followership, and for advocating the Followership Learning Community at ILA, have left a permanent marker on the landscape of followership studies. My thanks, too, to Shelly Wilsey and her staff at ILA for their continuous support. One of ILA's founders, Dr. Barbara Kellerman, of the John F. Kennedy School of Government at Harvard, has become a fellow toiler in the field of followership and has also done much for its advancement. Dr. Robert Kelley of Carnegie Mellon University, who wrote the original book on followership, also continues to lend his well-deserved reputation to the field. My special gratitude goes to my indefatigable coadministrator of the Followership Learning Community, Elisabeth Higgins Null.

Completing my immediate professional circle, I wish to acknowledge Georgetown University's Leadership Development Program and the Office of Personnel Management's Eastern Management Development Center for embracing the importance of courageous followership in their curricula. I am especially grateful to the good people at Berrett-Koehler who have partnered with me on this journey. Two Berrett-Koehler principals deserve special acknowledgment. Pat Andersen in her tenure at Berrett-Koehler was a tireless champion of this project from the moment she encountered it, and her enthusiasm kept wind beneath my wings. Steven Piersanti recognized the importance of this work in its rough, early stages and guided me in bringing out its full potential in each edition. It was my belief, and remains so, that he collaborates with the angels to do his work.

THE COURAGEOUS FOLLOWER SELF-ASSESSMENT

You may be interested in The Courageous Follower Self-Assessment companion product. This twenty-question online self-assessment is available at **www.bkconnection.com/courageousfollower-sa**.

Many instruments have been designed to capture and reflect leadership styles, but few exist to serve the same purpose for followership styles. Yet understanding our style and growth direction can be critical for our professional development and satisfaction in our work relationships.

Based on your responses, this self-assessment will provide you with language and descriptions about your follower style. It will display these visually and provide you with guidance about growth directions that you might choose to pursue. You may be interested in this assessment in preparation for a Courageous Follower workshop or simply to satisfy your own curiosity and desire for improvement. You may print out your customized followership profile and retake the self-assessment up to five times within a twelve-month period.

Discounts are available for organizational programs.

SELECT
BIBLIOGRAPHY

EPIGRAPH ON PAGE xi

The quote is from Baldesar Castiglione, *The Book of the Courtier*, translated by Charles S. Singleton (New York: Doubleday, Anchor Books, 1959).

PREFACE

The information about the Holocaust comes largely from two sources: Dr. Louis S. Snyder, *Encyclopedia of the Third Reich* (New York: Paragon House, 1989); and the United States Holocaust Memorial Museum, Washington, DC.

CHAPTER 1

THE COMMON PURPOSE AND CORE VALUES
For vivid historical studies of the relationships among leaders, followers, and purposes, I recommend Gary Wills, *Certain Trumpets: The Call of Leaders* (New York: Simon & Schuster, 1994).

WHO DOES A FOLLOWER SERVE?
An extensive examination of how the roles of servant and leader, or servant and follower, can be fused is found in Robert K. Greenleaf, *Servant Leadership: A Journey into the Nature of Legitimate Power and Greatness* (New York: Paulist Press, 1977).

For a comparably rich examination of service and the appropriate use of power, see Peter Block, *Stewardship: Choosing Service over Self-Interest* (San Francisco: Berrett-Koehler, 1993).

POWER IN THE LEADER-FOLLOWER RELATIONSHIP
I found a compelling discussion on the power to choose how we react—even in the horrific environment of a concentration camp—in Victor Frankl, *Man's Search for Meaning* (New York: Washington Square Press, 1959, 1984).

COURAGE OF THE FOLLOWER
For a profound and beautiful exploration of courage displayed before senior executives, read David Whyte, *The Heart Aroused: Poetry and the Preservation of the Soul in Corporate America* (New York: Currency Doubleday, 1994). The chapter "Fire in the Voice: Speaking Out at Work" is especially powerful.

FINDING EQUAL FOOTING WITH THE LEADER
I drew on a moving account of helping fellow sentient beings, regardless of their formal relationship to us, that I found in Ram Dass and Paul Gorman, *How Can I Help? Stories and Reflections on Service* (New York: Knopf, 1987).

CHAPTER 2

INTRODUCTION TO THE COURAGE TO ASSUME RESPONSIBILITY

For the most serious discussion I have found on the responsibility of followers, and for a good instrument to measure yourself by, see Robert E. Kelley, *Power of Followership: How to Create Leaders People Want to Follow and Followers Who Lead Themselves* (New York: Double Currency, 1991).

FOLLOWERSHIP STYLE

A book that was published contemporaneously with the first edition of *The Courageous Follower* and that adds greatly to the research and literature on followership styles and their relationship to authority is Gene Boccialetti, *It Takes Two: Managing Yourself When Working with Bosses and Other Authority Figures* (San Francisco: Jossey-Bass, 1995).

When the first edition of *The Courageous Follower* was published, few works were available on styles of followership other than the two works just mentioned. Happily, that situation is rapidly changing. Two of the recent works containing other models of followership style are *The Art of Followership: How Great Followers Create Great Leaders and Organizations*, edited by Ronald E. Riggio, Ira Chaleff, and Jean Lipman-Blumen (San Francisco: Jossey-Bass, 2008), which contains several additional models by contributing authors; and *Followership: How Followers Are Creating Change and Changing Leaders*, by Barbara Kellerman (Cambridge, MA: Harvard Business School Press, 2008). The model of followership in this work is based on follower activity level and is enriched by the author's political science framework.

ELICITING FEEDBACK

This book provides detailed process help on soliciting feedback from others: Mardy Grothe and Peter Wylie, *Problem Bosses: Who They Are and How to Deal with Them* (New York: Fawcett Crest, 1987).

SELF-MANAGEMENT

For an in-depth approach to improving personal organization, see the fourth edition of Kerry Gleeson, *The Personal Efficiency Program: How to Stop*

Feeling Overwhelmed and Win Back Control of Your Work (New York: Wiley, 2009).

INFLUENCING THE CULTURE
I am grateful to a client for recognizing the link between courageous followers and tempered radicals and sending me the following book. It makes the task of finding the thin line between conforming to and influencing organizational culture less lonely. Debra E. Meyerson, *Tempered Radicals: How People Use Difference to Inspire Change at Work* (Cambridge, MA: Harvard Business School Press, 2001).

TESTING YOUR IDEAS
For a dynamic view of using pilots to test ideas, see Tom Peters, *Thriving on Chaos: A Handbook for a Management Revolution* (New York: Knopf, 1987).

CHAPTER 3

PRESENTING OPTIONS
A thorough approach for examining assumptions is presented in Stephen D. Brookfield, *Developing Critical Thinkers* (San Francisco: Jossey-Bass, 1987).

A comprehensive process for situation appraisal, problem analysis, and decision analysis is contained in Charles H. Kepner and Benjamin B. Tregoe, *The New Rational Manager* (Princeton, NJ: Princeton Research Press, 1981).

I learned the rule of generating three options to assist in making ethical choices from Michael Josephson at the Josephson Institute of Ethics, Marina del Rey, California.

MANAGING CRISES
For a comprehensive review of preparing for crises, refer to Ian L. Mitroff and Thierry C. Pauchant, *Transforming the Crisis-Prone Organization* (San Francisco: Jossey-Bass, 1992).

WHEN THE LEADER IS ILL

I drew on a fascinating treatise on the rarely examined subject of illness in leaders by Jerrold M. Post and Robert S. Robins, "The Captive King and His Captive Court: The Psychopolitical Dynamics of the Disabled Leader and His Inner Circle 1," *Political Psychology* 11, no. 2 (June 1990): 331–352.

CHAPTER 4

OVERCOMING GROUPTHINK

The major work on this subject has been done by Irving L. Janis, *Group-think, Psychological Studies of Policy Decisions and Fiascoes* (Boston: Houghton Mifflin, 1972, 1982).

CHALLENGING THE USE OF LANGUAGE

The following book contains an important discussion on the power of language; it examines the problems of German psychotherapy patients whose families wouldn't talk about their role in World War II: *The Collective Silence*, edited by Barbara Heimannsberg and Christoph Schmidt (San Francisco: Jossey-Bass, 1992).

LEADERS WHO SCREAM

For a detailed process on how to comport oneself in the face of out-of-control screaming, listen to the section about bullying bosses on the tape by Robert Bramson, *Coping with Difficult Bosses* (New York: Simon & Schuster Audio, 1992).

CHAPTER 5

THE PROCESS OF PERSONAL TRANSFORMATION

A comprehensive and scholarly overview of the basic principles and processes of human psychological change is contained in Michael J. Mahoney, *Human Change Processes* (New York: Basic Books, 1991).

THE FOLLOWER'S ROLE
The literature on codependency contains important experience for those supporting a transformation process. The book I found most helpful as a resource is Melody Beattie, *Codependent No More: How to Stop Controlling Others and Start Caring for Yourself* (San Francisco: HarperCollins, 1987).

THE FOLLOWER AS CATALYST; DENIAL AND JUSTIFICATION OF BEHAVIOR; IDENTIFYING TRANSFORMATION RESOURCES
The most important work I am aware of on the practical application of personal development to executive performance problems is Robert E. Kaplan, *Beyond Ambition: How Driven Managers Can Lead Better and Live Better* (San Francisco: Jossey-Bass, 1991).

MODELING CHANGE FOR A LEADER
An interesting chapter on "Modeling Behavior: Helping Your Boss to Learn" appears in William P. Anthony, *Managing Your Boss* (New York: AMACOM, 1983).

MODELING EMPATHY
For one of the most profound discussions on denying vulnerability by victimizing others, see Ernst Becker, *Escape from Evil* (New York: Free Press, 1975).

CHAPTER 6

THE COURAGE TO TAKE MORAL ACTION
Extensive thought and research by Gene Dixon on the validity of the Courageous Follower model suggest, among other things, that the "Courage to Leave" is properly subsumed under the "Courage to Take Moral Action." This dissertation has been published as *An Exploration of the Effects of Organizational Behavior on Attributions of Followership* (Huntsville: University of Alabama Press, 2003). It includes a survey instrument for directly assessing courageous followership.

THREATENING TO RESIGN; IF WE DECIDE TO STAY

The original, brilliant thinking on this subject is found in the following book, which examines economic, political, and moral phenomena: Albert O. Hirschman, *Exit, Voice and Loyalty: Responses to Decline in Firms, Organizations, and States* (Cambridge, MA: Harvard University Press, 1970).

For a derivative but illustrative complement to Hirschman, see the chapter "Quitting on Principle" in Warren Bennis, *Why Leaders Can't Lead* (San Francisco: Jossey-Bass, 1989).

THE DECISION TO WITHDRAW SUPPORT; WHEN LEADERS MUST BE OPPOSED

A book that appeared after I wrote these chapters presents a powerful analysis of the nature of toxic leadership and what options must be weighed when the toxicity becomes evident to followers who were previously in the leader's thrall. See *The Allure of Toxic Leaders: Why We Follow Destructive Bosses and Corrupt Politicians—and How We Can Survive Them*, by Jean Lipman-Blumen (New York: Oxford University Press, 2005).

EVIL BEHAVIOR

I'm sure that there are endless books describing statistical distribution, but as a nonstatistician, I have used a book by Derek Rowntree, *Statistics without Tears: A Primer for Non-Mathematicians* (New York: Scribner's, 1981).

For a hard look at the phenomenon of group evil, read the chapter "My Lai: An Examination of Group Evil" in M. Scott Peck, *People of the Lie: The Hope for Healing Human Evil* (New York: Simon & Schuster, 1983).

CHAPTER 7

THE COURAGE TO SPEAK TO THE HIERARCHY

For a full discussion on the distinctions between hierarchical structure and hierarchical relationships, see Samuel A. Culbert and John B. Ullmen, *Don't Kill the Bosses! Escaping the Hierarchy Trap* (San Francisco: Berrett-Koehler, 2001).

The evolution from the bureaucratic social character to the interactive social character that is more peer focused than authority focused is examined by Michael Maccoby in *The Leaders We Need and What Makes Us Follow* (Cambridge, MA: Harvard Business School Press, 2007).

THE CHALLENGE OF MANY HANDS
The practice of "many hands" touching each piece of work in large bureaucracies, and the consequences of this reality on a sense of personal responsibility, is examined by Mark Bovens in *The Quest for Responsibility: Accountability and Citizenship in Complex Organizations* (Cambridge: Cambridge University Press, 1998).

FRAMING THE ISSUE TO COMMAND ATTENTION
For a sobering examination of why executives will ignore early indicators of potential disaster, see *Flirting With Disaster: Why Accidents Are Rarely Accidental*, by Marc Gerstein, with Michael Ellsberg (New York: Union Square Press, 2008).

CIRCUMVENTING THE HIERARCHY
The research I cite is described in an article that provides much-needed perspective by Jeffrey W. Kassing, "Going around the Boss: Exploring the Consequences of Circumvention," *Management Communication Quarterly* 21, no. 1 (August 2007): 55–74.

SPEAKING UP IN MULTILEVEL MEETINGS
The metaphor of lion taming has been very useful to a number of my clients who occasionally interact with senior leaders. See *Lion Taming: Working Successfully with Leaders, Bosses and Other Tough Customers*, by Steven L. Katz (Naperville, IL: Sourcebooks, 2004).

CHAPTER 8

INVITING CREATIVE CHALLENGE
For a marvelous discussion of how to create group norms that encourage people to speak out without fear, see Kathleen D. Ryan and Daniel K.

Oestreich, *Driving Fear Out of the Workplace* (San Francisco: Jossey-Bass, 1991).

While writing this book, I participated in a stimulating program that demonstrated how to create an environment that encourages truly creative thinking. It is called the Mind-Free Program, developed by Kathleen Logan Prince and George M. Prince of Weston, Massachusetts.

CREATING PROTECTED COMMUNICATION CHANNELS
In an exhaustive survey of the strengths and weaknesses of methods for improving accountability in large organizations, Mark Bovens argues effectively that leadership must create "safe harbors" for those reporting moral discomfort with corporate actions. Read *The Quest for Responsibility: Accountability and Citizenship in Complex Organizations* (Cambridge: Cambridge University Press, 1998).

DISCERNMENT: WHAT IS THE RIGHT ACTION?
For a historical and practical examination of discernment as it is employed in Quaker communities that may illuminate our own efforts to discern right action, see Patricia Loring, *Spiritual Discernment: The Context and Goal of Clearness Committees* (Wallingford, PA: Pendle Hill, 1992).

INDEX

ABOUT THE AUTHOR

 I CAME TO WASHINGTON, DC, in 1982, another in the never-ending chain of those who see this city as a vehicle for making a difference, large or small. I joined the staff of the Congressional Management Foundation (www.cmfweb.org), a nonprofit group that studies management in the U.S. Congress and offers training and consulting to improve existing practices, and subsequently became its executive director. Although the public view of Congress is not generally high, many dedicated individuals in the institution are trying to get the work of Congress done. I learned a lot about leader-follower relations from this experience and continued to serve as chairman of the foundation's board of directors while creating the third edition of this book. Occasionally, I get to apply this experience in helping legislators from other countries who are interested in strengthening the legislative branch of government in emerging democracies.

In 1987, I teamed up with Kerry Gleeson, the founder of the Institute for Business Technology (ww.ibt-pep.com), to open the U.S. branch of this international training and consulting organization. The company has a special niche: improving white-collar productivity at the level of the individual and small work group within the organization. This experience gave me the opportunity to work closely with hundreds of leaders and followers in the private and nonprofit sectors as they struggle with the practical elements of getting their jobs done in complex organizational settings.

The majority of my work currently is conducted through a consortium I founded in 1998 called Executive Coaching & Consulting Associates (www.exe-coach.com). This hand-picked group of diverse, highly talented men and women are a wonderful team of colleagues who continually learn from each other. We provide executive coaching and organization development services singly, in pairs, or in teams, matching our complementary talents to specific client needs. Many of the issues explored in this book come to life in coaching individual executives and management teams.

Since the publication of the first edition of *The Courageous Follower*, there has been a steady and growing request for workshops on the topic. In response, I have developed half-day, full-day, and multiple-day formats, including train-the-trainer programs (see www.courageousfollower.net). Thousands of participants have shared their experiences and reevaluated the way they perform their roles as both leader and follower in their organizational relationships.

In 2006, I cohosted the first national conference on followership in the United States at Claremont University. The book *The Art of Followership: How Great Followers Create Great Leaders and Organizations* grew out of this conference, an edited collection of scholarly and practitioner thought on the emerging field. In 2008, I launched the Followership Learning Community (http://followership2.pbwiki.com) under the auspices of the International Leadership Association (www.ila-net.org) , which is rapidly becoming the go-to site for updates in the field.

For those who prefer a do-it-yourself approach to improving the quality of followership in your organizations, I recommend the video and trainer's guide *Courageous Followers, Courageous Leaders: New Relationships for Changing Times* by CRM films (www.crmlearning.com). This award-winning video is based on the Courageous Follower model and can be used as a catalyst for team dialogue on leader-follower relations in many settings.

If you wish to contact me in any of these roles, please do so through the relevant website or through Berrett-Koehler's sites: www.bkconnection .com and www.bkconnection.com/authors.asp.

Berrett–Koehler
Publishers

Berrett-Koehler is an independent publisher dedicated to an ambitious mission: *Creating a World That Works for All*.

We believe that to truly create a better world, action is needed at all levels—individual, organizational, and societal. At the individual level, our publications help people align their lives with their values and with their aspirations for a better world. At the organizational level, our publications promote progressive leadership and management practices, socially responsible approaches to business, and humane and effective organizations. At the societal level, our publications advance social and economic justice, shared prosperity, sustainability, and new solutions to national and global issues.

A major theme of our publications is "Opening Up New Space." Berrett-Koehler titles challenge conventional thinking, introduce new ideas, and foster positive change. Their common quest is changing the underlying beliefs, mindsets, institutions, and structures that keep generating the same cycles of problems, no matter who our leaders are or what improvement programs we adopt.

We strive to practice what we preach—to operate our publishing company in line with the ideas in our books. At the core of our approach is stewardship, which we define as a deep sense of responsibility to administer the company for the benefit of all of our "stakeholder" groups: authors, customers, employees, investors, service providers, and the communities and environment around us.

We are grateful to the thousands of readers, authors, and other friends of the company who consider themselves to be part of the "BK Community." We hope that you, too, will join us in our mission.

A BK Business Book

This book is part of our BK Business series. BK Business titles pioneer new and progressive leadership and management practices in all types of public, private, and nonprofit organizations. They promote socially responsible approaches to business, innovative organizational change methods, and more humane and effective organizations.

Berrett–Koehler
Publishers

A community dedicated to creating
a world that works for all

Visit Our Website: www.bkconnection.com

Read book excerpts, see author videos and Internet movies, read our authors'
blogs, join discussion groups, download book apps, find out about the BK Affiliate
Network, browse subject-area libraries of books, get special discounts, and more!

Subscribe to Our Free E-Newsletter, the *BK Communiqué*

Be the first to hear about new publications, special discount offers, exclusive
articles, news about bestsellers, and more! Get on the list for our free e-newsletter
by going to **www.bkconnection.com**.

Get Quantity Discounts

Berrett-Koehler books are available at quantity discounts for orders of ten or more
copies. Please call us toll-free at (800) 929-2929 or email us at bkp.orders@
aidcvt.com.

Join the BK Community

BKcommunity.com is a virtual meeting place where people from around the world
can engage with kindred spirits to create a world that works for all. **BKcommunity
.com** members may create their own profiles, blog, start and participate in forums
and discussion groups, post photos and videos, answer surveys, announce and
register for upcoming events, and chat with others online in real time. Please join
the conversation!

SFI Certified Sourcing
www.sfiprogram.org
SFI-00453